LONDON ASSOCIATION OF CLASSICAL T

LACTOR 12

THE CULTURE
OF
ATHENS

EDITED BY

J. P. Sabben-Clare
and
M. S. Warman

THE CULTURE OF ATHENS

First Published   - June 1978

Reprinted   - 1980, 1985 (with corrections)

Reset and reprinted - September 1991 (with corrections)

ISBN: 0 903625 15 6

FOREWORD

The original plan of the LACTOR was to collect material by studying the references in *Athenian Culture and Society* by T. B. L. Webster. A team of translators set about examining the references and selecting what seemed relevant and useful to likely users of the LACTOR. As the resultant translations accumulated, it became evident that they would not in themselves form a comprehensive or balanced account of Athenian society, and that an editor was needed who could form an overall plan, independent of Webster, and accumulate additional material. James Sabben-Clare, who had already done much work on the subject, undertook this task and has made the final selection of material. Inevitably this has meant that the original translators (Hugh Amos, Margaret Birch, Pat Davies, Barbara Hodge, Bernard Marchant, Ian Pratt, Bob Skeat, David Taylor and myself) will find that much of their work has been omitted or truncated in the interests of balance and economy. Warm thanks are due to them for getting the project off the ground and supplying some of the freight: and hearty apologies for the painful need to jettison some of this freight after the first hop.

Feb. 1978   Mark Warman.

NOTES AND ABBREVIATIONS

Spelling. In an attempt to achieve consistency, the Latin spelling has been adopted for the names of people and most places (excluding islands ending in -os); however a stricter orthography is used where Greek terms are transliterated. No doubt inconsistencies may still be found, and apologies in advance are offered to the puristic.

Dates. All dates are BC unless otherwise specified.

Brackets. Some explanatory matter, e.g. dates, is included in the texts in italics within brackets.

Bibliography. No full bibliography is included, but several modern works are referred to in the context of specific topics and problems.

Abbreviations.

CA is prefixed to all the excerpts translated in this book.

AE refers to excerpts in LACTOR 1 (*The Athenian Empire*).

fl. = flourished: the date of principal activity.

dr. = drachma/drachmae

ob. = obols (6 obols = 1 drachma)

Collections of Inscriptions:

IG = *Inscriptiones Graecae*

SIG = *Sylloge Inscriptionum Graecarum* ed. Dittenberger

ML = *Greek Historical Inscriptions*, 2nd. edition by Meiggs and Lewis.

TABLE OF CONTENTS

6

INTRODUCTION

It is presumptuous to suggest that anyone could incorporate in a single volume all the source material needed for studying the culture of Athens. The subject is as wide as are the interests of civilised man, and the potential sources as numerous as the whole corpus of Classical literature. But to admit the impossibility of the task is not to say that it should not be attempted; only, if there is to be any chance of success, the odds have got to be bent a little first.

To bring the subject within the compass of this book, we have submitted to certain external limitations and deliberately imposed upon ourselves several more. The terminal dates are those of the JACT Ancient History syllabus, whose Culture of Athens subject concentrates on the second half of the fifth century only. This does not mean that all fourth-century literature is excluded; the book would be very thin without it, and several chapters would have disappeared altogether. We have been prepared to use anything that can reasonably be supposed to illustrate aspects of fifth-century life, even if it was written over a thousand years later.

The limitations on subject matter are determined in part by the existing volumes in the LACTOR series: the Athenian Empire and Athenian Politics are already covered in LACTORS 1 and 5, and no attempt is made, other than by cross-references, to treat them further in this book. Other restrictions are imposed by the subject-matter itself. Since we have limited ourselves to literary and epigraphic sources, we can only make a token gesture of acknowledgement towards the architectural and artistic achievements of the period. Nor have we attempted to evaluate the literary masterpieces of Tragedy and Comedy. Aristophanes and Euripides figure quite prominently in the text, but only to illustrate more general points, about religious ideas for instance, and the place of drama in Athenian society; to appreciate their worth as literature, the plays must be read in their entirety.

To reduce the bulk further, we have excluded from the excerpts certain authors whom we take to be easily available in other translations, and better read at greater length. The political pamphlet of the Old Oligarch is covered in LACTOR 2; other works relegated (reluctantly) to the footnotes are the *Histories* of Herodotus and Thucydides, and the dialogues of Plato contained in the Penguin Classic *The Last Days of Socrates*. Where relevant, reference to these works has been made, but no translation included.

This has still left an enormous field to choose form, and I am very much aware that for every passage chosen another ten have been passed over. Readers familiar with the subject already are bound to raise an eyebrow at the inclusion of this or that rather than the other. But in the final analysis the selection must be a personal one, further limited by the size of the book. At best it will form a nucleus of sources for others to add to from their own reading.

The Culture of Athens special subject has sometimes been called the main *raison d'être* of the JACT Ancient History syllabus. Its introduction in 1965 pointed the way towards the serious study of Classical civilisation from English texts, which now flourishes at every academic level. But for many teachers its difficulty and lack of definition still outweigh its obvious attractiveness. This volume is intended to redress the balance somewhat. To the London Association of Classical Teachers who invited me to take it on, bending their frontiers to include South Hampshire, I am humbly grateful. I am indebted to Mr. Justin Pinkess who has opportunely filled a vacuum by supplying the entire section on Music; and most particularly do I thank Mr. Mark Warman, my coadjutor, who has undertaken the translation of all the excerpts from Plato and Aristotle and the Orators, as well as editing translations from other contributors. The initial selection of passages, their arrangement and presentation, and the translation of over half of them, has been my task. For any errors and deficiencies that may be found in the volume as a whole, therefore, I cannot lightly palm off the responsibility onto others.

Feb. 1978   James Sabben-Clare
                                                               Winchester College

INDEX OF PASSAGES TRANSLATED

GREEK AUTHORS

NOTES ON AUTHORS

Names marked * also appear in the General Index at the end. The letters AE after a name show that further information may be found in the biographical index of LACTOR 1, *The Athenian Empire*, pp. xvi–xx.

GREEK AUTHORS

AELIAN (c. AD 170–235). Collector of miscellaneous information. AE.

AESCHINES (c.390–330). Orator and rival of Demosthenes. Speeches against Timocrates for corruption and immorality (1); against Ctesiphon for proposing that a crown be conferred on Demosthenes (3). AE.

AESCHYLUS (525–c. 456). Tragedian. AE.

AETIUS (?c. AD 100). Philosophical epitomist, containing excerpts from many lost works.

ALEXIS (c.372–270). Poet of Middle Comedy.

*ANAXAGORAS (c.500–428). Philosopher and friend of Pericles.

ANDOCIDES (c.440–after 390). Politician implicated in the Hermae affair. Speeches: on his return in 410, claiming immunity from religious exclusion (1); against Alcibiades, a non-contemporary forgery (4). AE.

*ANTIPHON (*the orator*) (fl. c.420–410). Oligarchic politician. Speeches 1–3 are rhetorical exercises containing speeches for the prosecution and defence in hypothetical cases. AE.

*ANTIPHON (*the sophist*) (fl.c.425). Known works include books on Truth, Politics and the Interpretation of Dreams.

APOLLONIUS RHODIUS (3rd. century BC). Alexandrian epic poet.

ARISTOPHANES (445–375). Comic poet. AE. (Also see AE for Scholiasts)

ARISTOTLE (384–322). Philosopher and polymath. AE.

ATHENAEUS (fl. AD 200). Litterateur from Egypt. His great work, the *Deipnosophists*, purports to be a series of dinner-party conversations illuminated by extensive quotations from earlier dramatic works, many of them since lost.

CLEMENT OF ALEXANDRIA (late 2nd. century AD). Christian convert, seeking to prove the superiority of Christianity to pagan religion.

*CRATINUS (c.480–420). Comic poet. Rival of Aristophanes.

CRITIAS (c.460–403). Sophist and politician. One of the Thirty; also a poet and tragedian.

DEMOSTHENES (384–322). Orator and politician. Many of the excerpts are from his speeches in private suits; they provide a great wealth of evidence about Athenian law and society, although some allowance must be made for the changes in situation since the end of the Peloponnesian War. AE.

DIODORUS SICULUS (fl.60–36). Historian. AE.

DIOGENES OF APOLLONIA (fl.c.425). Philosopher with particular interest in natural science.

DIOGENES LAERTIUS (3rd. century AD). Wrote a biographical history of philosophy.

DIONYSIUS OF HALICARNASSUS (fl.30–8). Antiquarian and literary historian. AE.

*EUPOLIS** (fl.430–412). Comic poet. Rival of Aristophanes. AE.

*EURIPIDES** (c.485–406). Tragedian. An innovator in dramatic form and content, and a mouthpiece for many new sophistic ideas.

EUSEBIUS (fl.c. AD 300). Christian Bishop of Caesarea.

EUSTATHIUS (12th. century AD). Literary scholar from Constantinople. His commentary on Homer incorporates material from lost Scholia and other works.

*GORGIAS** (c.483–376). Sophist and orator from Sicily. Developer and teacher of new rhetorical techniques.

GREEK ANTHOLOGY. A miscellaneous collection of epigrams accumulated from the 4th. century BC onwards.

HARPOCRATION (2nd. century AD). Lexicographer from Alexandria. AE.

HESYCHIUS (? 5th. century AD). Lexicographer from Alexandria.

*HIPPOCRATES** (c.470–400). Physician from Cos. The Hippocratic writings are mostly the work of members of his school but reflect the development of a more scientific approach to medicine in the 5th. and 4th. centuries.

HIPPOLYTUS (3rd. century AD). Ecclesiastical writer from Italy.

ISAEUS (c.420–350). Speech-writer, probably from Athens. All his extant speeches are concerned with matters of inheritance on which he was obviously an expert.

ISOCRATES (436–338). Orator and teacher. AE.

JULIAN (AD 331–363). Roman Emperor 361–3. A man of many talents and interests, reflected in his letters and other writings.

LUCIAN (c. AD 120–after 180). Writer and teacher on numerous subjects.

LYCURGUS (died 324). Politician and orator. His one extant speech attacks Leocrates on a charge of treachery.

LYSIAS (c.440–380). Speech-writer; the son of a wealthy Sicilian who had moved to Athens. As a metic he personally suffered in the Thirty's reign of terror in 404–3. AE.

LYSIPPUS (fl.c.425). Comic poet.

MARCELLINUS (? 6th. century AD). The collator of a number of earlier biographical works on Thucydides.

NICETAS (12th. century AD). Byzantine historian.

PAUSANIAS (c. AD 115–180). Traveller and Antiquarian. AE.

PHERECRATES (fl.c.425). Comic poet.

PHILEMON (c.361–262). Poet of New Comedy.

PHILOPONUS (6th. century AD). Commentator on Aristotle.

PLATO (*the comic poet*) (fl.c.400). Writer of comedies of Old and Middle type.

PLATO (c.429–347). Philosopher. His experience of Socrates' teaching and reaction to his execution led him first to perpetuate in his writings the memory of his teacher, and then to develop his philosophical ideas. Although his dialogues are set in the 5th. century, their testimony, on educational matters in particular, is weighted with Plato's own prejudices against sophists and other opponents of Socrates.

PLATONIUS (date unknown). Wrote on the difference between Old, Middle and New Comedy.

PLUTARCH (c. AD 46–120). Essayist and biographer from Chaeronea. In addition to the *Lives*, comparing Greek and Roman notables, he wrote a large number of essays on ethical, religious, political and artistic subjects. AE.

POLLUX (2nd. century AD). His glossary of technical terms (on many different subjects) is preserved in a 10th.-century epitome.

PRATINAS. Dithyrambic poet, perhaps different from and later than the writer of satyr plays of that name known to us from the beginning of the 5th. century BC.

PRODICUS (fl.c.425). Sophist from Ceos, mainly interested in semantics.

SEXTUS EMPIRICUS (late 2nd. century AD). His work *Against The Teachers* criticises the teaching of non-philosophical subjects, and contains excerpts from works since lost.

SOPHOCLES (c.496–406). Tragedian. His plays are structurally more complex than those of Aeschylus, but reflect the same religious orthodoxy.

THEMISTIUS (4th. century AD). Commentator on Aristotle.

THEOPHRASTUS (c.370–285). Pupil of Aristotle. Writer on scientific subjects, including the sketches of human types in his *Characters*.

THRASYMACHUS (fl.c.420). Sophist and rhetorician from Chalcedon.

TIMOTHEUS (c.450–360). Innovatory dithyrambic poet from Miletus.

XENOPHON (c.425–355). Soldier and writer, who migrated to Sparta. The works chiefly used here are the *Memorabilia* – a defence of Socrates and record of his opinions, probably at least based on reality; and *Economicus*, a treatise on estate-management drawn from his own experience. For his *Poroi (Revenues)* see AE.

ROMAN AUTHORS

CICERO (106–43). His non-political writings include works on oratory and the Stoic philosophy.

JUVENAL (c. AD 50–130). Satirist.

PLINY THE ELDER (AD 23–79). His *Natural History* is an encyclopaedic work uncritically compiled from over 100 authors.

QUINTILIAN (c. AD 35–100). Teacher and writer on rhetoric.

VITRUVIUS (end of 1st. century BC). Architect and military engineer.

CA1 CICERO, *Pro Flacco* 62

> There are men here from Athens, the city which is regarded as having produced humanity, learning, religion, crops, justice and laws, and distributed them throughout the world.

CA 2 LYSIPPUS, fr. 7

> If you haven't seen Athens, you're a blockhead. If you've seen it and not been captivated, you're an ass. If you're glad to get away from it, you're a pack-ass.

I. ATTICA

(a) NATURAL RESOURCES

The territory of Attica covers the same area as a medium-sized English County, with a maximum distance of about 50 miles from end to end and from side to side. Much of it is mountainous, and as the rainfall is the lowest of anywhere in Greece only a quarter of it is cultivable. The climate is mild and this permits a long growing season, but the long summer drought allows few main crops to flourish except the hardy olive; the raptures of the Comic writers must be set alongside Thucydides' contention (1.2.3–6) that the very poverty of the Attic soil was responsible for her political stability: it simply wasn't worth fighting over. The wealth of Attica lay in her mineral resources (the silver, the building stone, the potter's clay), her harbour at Piraeus, and above all in the character of her people.

CA 3 PLATO, *Critias* 110e–111d

> Compelling evidence of the virtue of the soil of ancient Attica is the fact that what remains of it now can vie with any soil in point of fertility in
>
> 111 every crop and pasturage for every animal. In olden times apart from its beauty it produced all these things in abundance. How can we justify this claim and the claim that the present soil is a relic of the old? Well, the whole country extends a long way into the sea like a promontory, and the basin of the sea round it is deep close in shore. During the many big floods
>
> b in the 9000-year period between now and then, the soil which was washed away from the heights did not form any significant deposit of silt, as happened elsewhere, but always flowed away all round into the deep water and disappeared: and there have been left, as in small islands, the bones, as it were, of an ailing body, all the rich and soft earth having been washed away, leaving only the wasted frame of the land. But in the old days when
>
> c the land was intact its mountains were earth-covered crests and the now rocky plains of Phelleus were covered with rich earth, and there was abundant forest on the mountains, of which there are still clear indications: some of the mountains which nowadays can support only bees not so long ago produced roof timbers for large buildings whose roofs are still sound. And there were many other cultivated trees and boundless pasturage for herds. Furthermore the land used profitably its yearly water
>
> d supply from Zeus and did not, as now, lose it by its draining off the thin

soil into the sea. Instead it had plenty of soil and took the water into this and stored it in the protecting clay, taking the water which drained off the heights into hollow regions everywhere and so providing a boundless supply for springs and rivers; and the shrines still remaining near old fountains are evidence of the truth of the theory.

CA 4 XENOPHON, *Memorabilia* 3.5.25

(*Socrates in conversation with the younger Pericles on the degeneracy of Athens*) (cf. LACTOR 5 p.44)

"You see, Pericles, how our country is barricaded by great mountains, which extend into Boeotia and have steep and narrow passes into our country, and how the interior is also circled with steep mountains."

CA 5 ARISTOPHANES, *Farmers (fr. 109, 110)*

109 O Peace, deep in riches, O my pair of oxen, if only I could cease from war, and dig and prune; then bathe and eat my bread and dressed salad, with draughts of new wine.

110 O dear city of Cecrops, native Attica; hail gleaming land, with fine rich soil.

CA 6 ARISTOPHANES, *Islands (fr. 387)*

O fool, fool, you've got everything here – a life of ease on your small-holding, free from the bother of the agora, with your very own pair of oxen, where you can hear the sound of bleating flocks, and of the grape-juice as it is pressed out into the vat; where you can feed on finches and thrushes, and not have to queue in the agora for very expensive fish, three days old and well thumbed by the rascally fishmonger.

CA 7 ARISTOPHANES, *Seasons (fr. 569. 1–8)*

In the middle of the winter you will see cucumbers, grapes, fruit, garlands of violets, roses, lilies, a blinding storm of blossom. The same man sells thrushes, pears, honeycombs, olives, beestings, haggis, russet figs, cicadas, embryos. You can see baskets snowed under with figs and myrtles. Then they plant gourds at the same time as turnips, so that nobody knows what time of year it is. There is no greater blessing than being able to get what you want all the year round.

CA 8 SOPHOCLES, *Oedipus at Colonus* 668–719

668 CHORUS OF OLD MEN OF ATTICA. You have come, friend, to the finest settlement in this land, rich in horses – white Colonus, where the clear-voiced nightingale trills from its haunt in the green shadows of the wood, among the wine-dark ivy and the sunless foliage, rich in berries, inaccessible to any but the god, and sheltered from the storms; where Dionysus ever holds his Bacchic revels with the godly nymphs as
681 companions. And ever a day flourishes in heavenly dew the beauteous

cluster of the narcissus, ancient crown for the great gods, and the golden gleam of the crocus; and never-resting, never-failing the meandering streams of Cephisus cover with their unpolluted tide the plains of this hillocky land, daily speeding the crops' growth. Nor have the

694   Muses' choruses spurned it, nor Aphrodite of the golden reins. There is a plant which flourishes mightily in this land – the like of none that I have heard of in Asia or the great Peloponnese – ever budding, immortal, self-renewing, the despair of enemy weapons, the grey-leafed olive, nurse of the young; no-one whether old or young will lay hands on it to destroy it; for the eye of Zeus, guardian of the sacred olives, and

708   grey-eyed Athena ever watch over them. And further great praise have I to tell of this mother-city, a gift of the great god, greatest pride of this land, pride in horses and foals, pride in its seas. O son of Cronus, lord Poseidon, you brought the land to this glory, introducing the bridle first in these roadways to master the horse. And the oar that fits well in the hand leaps wondrously over the sea, following the fifty dancing Nereids.

CA 9 ARISTOTLE, *Constitution of Athens* 16.2–6

2   Pisistratus managed the city's affairs with moderation and more like a constitutional ruler than a tyrant. He was generally kind and lenient and forgiving, and in particular he lent money to the poor for their farming so

3   that they could get a living from the soil. He did this for two reasons, first to keep them scattered in the countryside rather than spend their time in Athens, secondly in order that having a reasonable subsistence and being occupied with their private concerns they should neither wish nor have

4   time to take an interest in politics. He also found his revenues increased by

5   the working of the land, since he took a tithe on all produce. For this reason he also set up boards of judges in the demes and himself often went on tours of inspection in the countryside, settling disputes, to prevent people coming to Athens for settlement and neglecting the land.

6   It was on one such tour they say, that there occurred the episode with the man who was farming the part of Hymettus later called the 'untaxed region'. Pisistratus saw the man digging and trying to cultivate sheer rock, and in his amazement asked his slave to enquire what the region produced.

    "Evils and pains of every kind," said the farmer, "and Pisistratus ought to take a tithe of them." He said this without realising who Pisistratus was, but Pisistratus was delighted with his frankness and his hard work and made him exempt from all tax.

CA 10 XENOPHON, *Poroi (Revenues)* 1.2–8

2   I was struck by the fact that our country is by nature able to bring in very substantial revenues. To give you proof of this, I will describe the

3   resources of Attica. The produce itself is evidence of the extreme mildness of the climate: crops are obtained from plants which in many other countries are not even able to germinate. The sea around the coasts is also

4   highly productive – just like the land. What is more, the seasonal produce provided by the gods here begins very early and finishes very late. And this supremacy is not just limited to annual crops, but to permanent resources as well; the land has stone in abundance, from which the finest temples and altars are made, and the most beautiful statues for the gods. It is in

5   great demand among Greeks and foreigners too. There is also land which produces nothing when sown, but when quarried can provide for many times more than if it grew corn. The silver below the surface is clearly providential; for not even a small vein of ore carries on into any of the numerous states that border on Attica by land or sea.

6   It would be reasonable for anyone to suppose that this city occupies just about the middle of Greece – and indeed of the whole world. For the further you go away from it, the greater extremes of heat and cold you meet. And if you want to travel from one end of Greece to the other, you cannot help going past Athens, on sea or on land, like the centre of a

7   circle. Furthermore, though she is not in fact surrounded by sea, winds from every quarter enable her to import what she needs and export what she wants, as if she were an island. For she is between two seas. Likewise her position on the mainland makes her a centre for land-borne com-

8   merce. Most states are troubled by barbarians on their borders; but the Athenians have as neighbours states who are themselves very far from any barbarians.

CA 11 XENOPHON, *Poroi (Revenues)* 4.2–3

2   The silver ore has been mined and quarried for years, but see how large the hills of unmined ore still look beside the heaps of waste thrown up by the

3   workings. In fact the silver-bearing area is evidently not being reduced, but continually being extended.

(b) IMPORTS

Attica was not self-supporting, and was fortunate to possess in Piraeus the largest and best protected harbour in Greece. This not only provided a base for the war-fleet that kept the Empire together but also attracted commerce from all over the Mediterranean basin. The content of trade was determined largely by the interest of individual merchants, many of them metics, and upon them therefore depended the provisioning of Athens. Certainly the State took steps to encourage and protect essential imports like corn and timber (for which see Old Oligarch 2.11–12, LACTOR 2 p.7) and regulated the conduct of trade within the City, but there was no overall state policy for balancing imports against exports, or even for guaranteeing necessary supplies. If there had been, the Spartans might have found it harder to reduce Athens to starvation in 404.

CA 12 PAUSANIAS 1.1.2

Piraeus was a settlement from antiquity, but not a port until Themistocles held office at Athens. Phalerum, where the sea is nearest to the city, was their port ... When Themistocles took office, as Piraeus appeared to him

to project as a more suitable place for shipping, and had three harbours instead of the one at Phalerum, he organised this as their port.

CA 13 ISOCRATES 4.42

The city established Piraeus as a trading-centre in the middle of Greece, of such magnitude that individual items which are difficult to obtain from different individual sources can all be provided with ease from there.

(This observation may well be derived from Thucydides 2.38.2 (Pericles' Funeral Speech). For a detailed list of imports see the Hermippus fragment in LACTOR 5 p.10)

CA 14 XENOPHON, *Poroi (Revenues)* 3.1–2

1   I will now say something to show that Athens is a very pleasant and profitable place to trade with. In the first place, I suppose, it has the finest and safest accommodation for ships, where those who have run into port

2   can ride at anchor without fear in spite of bad weather. Moreover in the majority of states traders are obliged to take away some cargo in return – for they cannot use coinage outside its country of origin; but from Athens merchants may take away in exchange a great many different things which people need, or if they do not wish to take any goods as exchange-cargo, they may do good business in taking silver; for wherever they sell this they always receive a higher price than they gave.

CA 15 XENOPHON, *Economicus* 20.27–28

(Socrates compares Ischomachus' father's love of agriculture with the merchant's love of corn)

27   "Merchants sail to any place where they hear there is a large quantity of

28   corn. They cross the Aegean, the Black Sea and the Sicilian sea; then, taking as much as they can, they carry it over the sea, in the same ship as they sail in themselves. And when they need money, they do not unload the corn wherever they happen to be, but take it wherever they hear it is most in demand."

CA 16 DEMOSTHENES 20.31–32

31   You are well aware that we eat more imported corn than any other country. Now the total corn we import from all other markets is matched by the corn that comes in from the Black Sea alone. And this is natural, not only because this region is richest in corn, but also because Leucon is in a position there to give special exemption to importers to Athens and to

32   decree priority for them in loading. And just look what this means. He charges to others who export from him a duty of one thirtieth. Now Athens takes from him about 400,000 medimni *(an Attic medimnus was about 52 litres, or 1$\frac{3}{8}$ bushels)* as you can see from the record kept by the Corn Board. So he is in effect giving us 10,000 for every 300,000.

(Leucon was King of Bosporus 393–353; in return for his services to Athens, he and his three sons were made Athenian citizens. For earlier Athenian

interest in the corn-trade with the Black Sea, see the Methone Treaty (ML 65 = AE 159))

CA 17 DEMOSTHENES 35.50–51

50   You know, gentlemen, how severe the law is if any Athenian carries a cargo of corn to anywhere other than Athens, or lends money for any trading centre other than at Athens...

51   (*Quotation of Law*) No Athenian or metic living in Athens, nor any of their subordinates, shall lend out money on a ship which is not going to carry corn to Athens.

CA 18 ARISTOTLE, *Constitution of Athens* 51.3–4

3   There used to be five Corn-Wardens elected by lot, five for the City and five for Piraeus... They see to it that unground corn goes on sale in the market for a fair price, then that the millers relate the selling-price of barley-meal to that of the barley, and that the bakers relate the price of bread to that of wheat, and that they use the standard weights, as legally

4   determined by the Corn-Wardens. They also elect by lot ten Trade-Superintendents: their job is to supervise the trading centre and to compel merchants to bring into the City two thirds of the corn they import for the Corn Exchange.

CA 19 XENOPHON, *Poroi (Revenues)* 5.3–4

3   When the city is peaceful, who would not desire it, beginning with ship-owners and traders? Surely those who are rich in corn and wine would do so. And what about those rich in oil and flocks, and those who are able to

4   make money by investment, using money intelligently? And indeed craftsmen and sophists and philosophers, and the poets and those who study their works, and the people who are eager for any sacred or profane things which are worth seeing and hearing? Not to mention the men who need to buy and sell a lot of goods quickly – where would they find their requirements better met than at Athens?

II. SOCIETY

(a) THE CITIZEN BODY

1. Population (CA 20–21)

There can be no certainty about the total population of 5th.-century Athens, but there is enough information in the sources about the number of citizens (adult males) to give us a reasonable idea. The most detailed information (though still very incomplete) is Thuc.2.13.6–8: at the start of the war in 431 Athens had 13,000 hoplites, and a further 16,000 of the 'oldest and youngest' on guard duty, 1200 cavalry and 1600 archers. For further discussion see A.W. Gomme: *Historical Commentary on Thucydides* ad loc., A. H. M. Jones:

Athenian Democracy pp. 161–5, and Webster: *Athenian Culture and Society* pp. 39–41.

CA 20 ARISTOTLE, *Constitution of Athens* 22.7

> In the archonship of Nicomedes (*483*), when the Maronea mines were discovered, and from the workings there was a surplus of 100 talents for the state, some people proposed that the silver should be distributed to the people (*dêmos*), but Themistocles prevented it.

Herodotus 7.144 says that such a distribution would have given each man 10 drachmas, suggesting a total citizen population of 60,000. But in 5.97 he gives the number as 30,000.

CA 21 XENOPHON, *Memorabilia* 3.6.14

> *Socrates is discussing with Glaucon problems of statesmanship, including that of keeping the city supplied with corn in an emergency.*

> "Our city consists of more than 10,000 homes, and it is difficult to look after so many households at once."

2. Class Structure (CA 22–23)

In spite of political equality Athenian society was not classless. The traditional nobility of the Eupatridae (= well-born) had been superseded in the early 6th. century by an aristocracy of wealth. This classification by property had ceased to have much formal importance by the time of Pericles, but even so many writers recognised how much social status was affected by wealth. Euripides *Suppliants* 229–245 (LACTOR 5 p.3) speaks of three classes of citizens: the useless rich, the dangerous poor, and the stabilising middle class; and the whole of the Old Oligarch's argument is based upon an assumption of a class-struggle between the poor majority and the rich minority (see especially 1.2–5, LACTOR 2 p.1–2). These ideas are developed at greater length in Aristotle's *Politics*.

CA 22 ARISTOTLE, *Politics* 1279b–1280a

> ... The real differentia between democracy and oligarchy is wealth not numbers: wherever government is based on wealth, whether a minority or a majority govern, that is oligarchy: wherever the poor govern, that is democracy. It so happens ... that the rich are few and the poor many.

CA 23 ARISTOTLE, *Politics* 1295b–1296a

> In all cities there are three divisions – the very wealthy, the very poor and those between. And since it is agreed that the moderate and middle way is the best, it is clear that this rule applies to the ownership of the good things of life. People who are blessed with a moderate amount of these things are the most likely to listen to reason, which is not true of those who are very handsome or very strong or very blue-blooded or very rich, or their opposite, the very poor, the very weak and the completely unprivileged;

the former actuated by arrogance trample on morality on a grand scale, the latter actuated by malice become petty villains. The middle class moreover are the least liable either to dodge office or to seek it excessively, – both attitudes damaging to society. Then the very fortunate in the way of strength, wealth, friends and suchlike, are neither willing to be governed nor understand the process (this starts at home when they are children and their comfortable style of life makes them undisciplined even at school), while those who are excessively deprived of all these things are excessively humble; so the latter do not know how to govern but only how to practise a slavish subservience, while the former do not know how to obey any controlling authority but only how to exert despotic rule. So you get a city of envious slaves and arrogant masters, not of free men. All this is far from friendship and political sharing; for sharing is a mark of friendship. People are unwilling to share even a journey with their enemies. . . .

It is clear that political sharing is most effective when it takes place through the middle class, and the best constitution is possible in cities where the middle class is large and more powerful, preferably than both the other classes, if not, than one, when it can add its support to the weaker party and create a balance and prevent extremes either way. Either extreme is liable to produce tyranny.

1296a   It is clear that the middle form of constitution is best. It alone is free from faction, thanks to the large middle element. And thus big cities are more free from faction than small because in small cities a complete split between rich and poor, with no middle element, is more likely to occur. For the same reason democracies are more secure and long-lasting than oligarchies: more people take a larger part in office because of the large middle class. If, without a middle-class, the poor become powerful, the result is speedy disaster.

3. Upper and Middle Classes (CA 24–34)

The most general term for designating members of an upper social class at Athens was *kaloikagathoi* (= fine and good men, or gentlemen). Wealth was a necessary criterion for membership (except in unusual cases like Socrates), but not a sufficient one; good breeding was also helpful but not essential. What mattered most was the way a man behaved, what he did with his money, what his interests were, and his attitudes to politics and his fellow men (see G.E.M. de Ste. Croix: *The Origins of the Peloponnesian War* pp.371–6). Some action might be merely symbolic, like the wearing of grasshopper hair-clips (Thuc. 1.6.3, Aristophanes *Clouds* 984, CA 325); others were deliberately designed to win prestige for political ends, by conspicuous expenditure on behalf of the state – notably in the case of Nicias, and Alcibiades (Thuc. 6.16. 1–3).

CA 24 XENOPHON, *Economicus* 11.9

(Socrates is questioning Ischomachus about the life of a gentleman)

"So you concern yourself with ways of getting rich and having a lot of money so that you have a lot of trouble looking after it."

"Certainly I concern myself with what you say. What I enjoy is honouring the gods on a generous scale, helping my friends if they need anything, and seeing that the city does not go unadorned for lack of money so far as I can."

CA 25 XENOPHON, *Economicus* 2.3–6

3   "I reckon" said Socrates, "that if I could find a good buyer, my house and all my possessions would fetch 5 minas quite easily; but I haven't any doubt at all that yours would fetch more than a hundred times as much."

4   "But in spite of that opinion you claim not to be short of money yourself, and pity me for my poverty."

"Certainly, for I have got enough to satisfy my wants; but you, with the life-style in which you are involved, and with your public reputation, you wouldn't have enough even if your possessions were three times their present size."

5   "Really? How do you make that out?" said Critobulus.

"First I see that you have to offer many substantial sacrifices, if you are not to offend both men and gods. Then you are expected to entertain many guests – and lavishly too; then you have to give dinners to other

6   citizens and treat them well, if you are to command any support. And furthermore I see that the state already imposes considerable obligations on you, making you pay for the keeping of horses, the training of choruses and gymnastic teams, and putting you in charge of other operations; what is more, if a war breaks out, I know that they will demand from you trierarchies and capital levies of a size which you will find difficult to manage. And wherever you fail to come up to the mark, I know that the Athenians will punish you as severely as if they had caught you stealing their property."

(For trierarchies and other public services ("liturgies"), see LACTOR 5 pp.50–52; also Index under "liturgy")

CA 26 XENOPHON, *Memorabilia* 1.1.16

Socrates' conversation was always about human affairs, investigating the nature of piety and impiety, good and bad, justice and injustice, sense and madness, bravery and cowardice, the state and the statesman, government and the governor, and everything else a knowledge of which he reckoned entitled you to call a man a gentleman, and ignorance of which, a mindless automaton (*literally 'slavish'*).

CA 27 XENOPHON, *Memorabilia* 1.2.29

When Socrates saw that Critias was in love with Euthydemus and that he was behaving as if he wanted to gratify his physical urges, he tried to dissuade him, saying that such conduct was servile and unfitting for a gentleman: he was no better than a beggar, making improper requests and entreaties of his loved one – on whom he was trying also to make a good impression.

(Paying court to handsome boys was one of the distinctive activities of the upper class. See CA 104ff.; also the numerous ornamental vases inscribed "So-and-so the Beautiful")

CA 28 PLUTARCH, *Nicias* 3.1–2

1
2   Nicias was inferior (to Pericles) in other gifts, but outstripped him in wealth; so he tried to lead the people by this means. Not having the confidence to confront Cleon's affability and ribaldry which enabled him to manipulate the Athenians at will, he began to win the support of the people by financing dramatic choruses and athletic training and ambitious displays of this sort, outdoing his predecessors and his contemporaries in extravagance and refinement.

In an age when most economic activities were on a very modest scale and profit margins small, it was difficult to make money without having substantial capital to start with. This in itself helps to explain why money-lending was one of the few really profitable businesses. The excerpt that follows is a summary of the finances of Demosthenes' father. Even though the business is reckoned to be a large one, it can be seen that more capital is tied up in simple cash investment than in the two factories.

CA 29 DEMOSTHENES 27.9–11

9   The size of the estate is clear even on this evidence. For on fifteen talents the assessment is three talents, and this was the tax agreed. But your knowledge will be even more exact if I give you the estate itself in detail. My father left two workshops, each doing a sizeable business; 32 or 33 cutlers worth 5 or 6 minas each, and others worth not less than 3 each from which he received a yearly income of 30 minas nett; and 20 couch-makers given as a pledge for 40 minas, who brought in 12 minas nett. He left about a talent in money, loaned out at 12%, on which the yearly
10 interest was more than 7 minas. All this he left as capital bringing a return ... the sum of the capital being 4 talents 5000 drachmas, and the yearly interest 50 minas. Apart from this, he left the ivory and iron which they worked and the bed-timber, worth about 80 minas; dye and bronze bought for 70 minas; a house worth 3000 drachmas, together with furniture, goblets, gold ornaments and my mother's dresses in all worth
11 about 10,000 drachmas; and 80 minas in cash. So much for what he left in home belongings. Apart from this he had 70 minas lent on bottomry, lodged with Xuthus; 2,400 drachmas banked with Pasion, 600 with Pylades, 1,600 with Demomeles; and loaned to various people in sums of 200 or 300 drachmas a total of about a talent. The sum of all these is more than 8 talents 50 minas: and you will find the grand total is around 14 talents.

CA 30 DEMOSTHENES 33.4

For some time now, gentlemen, I have been engaged in maritime business; for a while I risked sailing in person, but it is now seven years since I gave that up; and now I try to make use of the moderate amount of capital that I have on maritime loans.

(The speaker, opposing the merchant Apaturius, is not identified)

The existence of a recognised class of parasites suggests that there was a certain amount of surplus wealth in Athens, at any rate before the Peloponnesian War.

CA 31 ATHENAEUS 6.236e

The old poets used to call parasites "flatterers"; this gave Eupolis the name of one of his plays, in which he makes the chorus of flatterers say (= *fr. 159*): "We'll tell you the way of life we flatterers have ... I have a nice pair of cloaks, and choose one or other of them when I sally forth to the agora. And when I see a man there with more money than brains, I'm all over him at once. And if this moneybags happens to say anything, I praise it for all I'm worth, and look as if I'm absolutely overcome with delight at his words. Then we go off to dinner, each one to a different table, not his own, where the flatterer has got to start making amusing conversation straight away, or he's out on his ear."

The plot of Aristophanes' *Clouds* provides us with an instance of conflict between upper and middle class interests. Megacles is a name suggestive of the old aristocracy, and Phidippides' passion for expensive equestrian pursuits identifies him with the upper class of any age. By contrast Strepsiades, an independent farmer like other heroes of Aristophanes' plays, exemplifies the homely conservatism of the middle class.

CA 32 ARISTOPHANES, *Clouds* 42–48, 60–67

42   STREPSIADES. To hell with the match-maker who got me to marry your
      mother. I used to have a lovely rustic life, all mildewed and dusty and
      chaotic, stuffed full of bees and sheep and olive-cakes. Then I, the
      country boy, went and married a city lady, the niece of Megacles, son of
      Megacles, a real toffee-nosed la-di-da Grande Dame ...

60   ... And when this son of ours was born to us, we had a row there and
      then about what to call him. She was all for some horsy name, like
      Xanthippus, or Charippus or Callippides; I wanted to give him the
      name of his grandfather Phidonides. So we went on arguing, till finally
      we compromised and called him Phidippides.

CA 33 XENOPHON, *Economicus* 5.1

"Not even the most prosperous can keep away from farming" said Socrates. "For it seems to be an occupation that provides a source of pleasure as well as a means of increasing one's estate and training one's body to undertake all that is fitting for a free man."

Peace was a necessary condition for the pursuit of this ideal. War brought the recurring threat of Spartan invasion and devastation. No wonder that the farmers in Aristophanes express the desire for peace in such fervent tones.

CA 34 ARISTOPHANES, *Peace* 551–600

551 TRYGAEUS. Hear ye, hear ye: the farmers may take up their farm
      implements and go off to the fields with all speed, leaving the spear, the

sword and the javelin. Everything here is now full of peace – and compost; let everyone go back to work in the fields, singing paeans.

556 CHORUS OF FARMERS. This is the day that honest farmers have longed for. How lovely to address myself to my vines, how I'm longing to greet the fig-trees I planted when I was younger after all this time.

560 TRYGAEUS. First my friends, let us pray to the goddess who removed the helmet-crests and the Gorgons; then let's buy some salt fish for the farm, and slip away home to our estates . . .

566 . . . Ye Gods, the mattock glints, all ready for action, and the fork gleams in the sun. They'll do a good job clearing the weeds from between the vines. How I long to get into the fields myself and break up my little plot of land with a pick. But my friends, remember the life of old that peace once gave us, the dried fruits, the figs and myrtles, the sweet new wine, the violet-bed by the well, the olives we love; for all these, worship the Peace-goddess here.

582 CHORUS. Welcome dearest one; how glad we are to see you! I am overwhelmed by desire for you, longing to creep back to the country. You were always the loved one, you brought the greatest profits for all of us who passed the life of the farmer; for you alone help us. Many the dear sweet things we enjoyed once in your time – and they cost us nothing. To the farmers you brought ears of wheat and salvation. So will the little vines and the new fig-shoots and all the other plants laugh as they welcome you with open arms.

4. Middle and Lower Classes (CA 35–38)

Most of the Athenians who lived and worked in the city were small-scale manufacturers and traders. Whether they were regarded as lower class or not would depend on their education, their attitudes and their occupation, as well as their financial status.

CA 35 XENOPHON, *Memorabilia* 3.7.6

Socrates encourages Charmides to become an active politician (cf. CA 424)

"Are you shy of the fullers and the cobblers, the builders, the blacksmiths and the farmers, the traders and people who engage in barter in the market and concentrate on buying cheap and selling at a profit? For it is people like that who make up the Assembly."

CA 36 XENOPHON, *Economicus* 4.2–3

2   Socrates said: "Yes, Critobulus, the so-called banausic occupations are always being disparaged, and, as you would expect, are very poorly regarded in our states. For they ruin the physique of the workmen and foremen, making them spend the day sitting indoors, away from the sunlight, sometimes even by the furnace. And as the physique is softened,
3   so is the mind also much enfeebled. Such occupations also mean that people have no time for attending to their friends or the state."

CA 37 ARISTOPHANES, *Knights* 177–189

177 DEMOS. You shall become, as this oracle says, a Very Great Man.

SAUSAGE-SELLER. Tell me how I, a mere sausage-seller, can become a man like that.

180   DEMOS. That's just what will make you great, the fact that you are a bare-faced rascal from the agora.

SAUSAGE-SELLER. But I don't have any pretensions to greatness.

DEMOS. Oh dear me, what's this about pretensions? Is it your conscience
185   or something? Surely you're not one of the gentry?

SAUSAGE-SELLER. Certainly not. I come from the lower orders (*ponêroi*).

DEMOS. What a stroke of luck! That's a great advantage in politics.

SAUSAGE-SELLER. But my friend, I haven't got any education (*mousikê*) except my letters, and I don't know them at all well.

CA 38 ARISTOPHANES, *Knights* 211–232

211   SAUSAGE-SELLER. But I can't think how a person like me could govern the people.

DEMOS. There's nothing to it. Just carry on as you're doing now. Stir
215   things up and make mincemeat of them all. Sweeten the people and win them over with your butcher's patter. You've got all the qualities of the demagogue, a loud voice, low birth, and the manners of the market.
222   You've got all it takes for politics . . . So take your stand against that man (*Cleon*).

SAUSAGE-SELLER. And who will stand by me? The rich are afraid of him and the poor are terrified.

225   DEMOS. But there are a thousand Knights, good men and true, who hate him; they will help you, along with any citizen who is a gentleman, and anyone in the audience who has any spirit – as well as the god and
230   myself. And don't be scared: he's not true to life, because the prop-makers were too frightened to do him life-like.

(See also LACTOR 5 p.22)

5. The Effect of the Peloponnesian War (CA 39–42)

The Peloponnesian War and its aftermath brought many changes in social attitudes. It was the wealthy who suffered most, from the devastation of their country property, and from the increasing burden of taxation and liturgies to finance the war as public funds ran out. For the first time some of the gentry found themselves having to work for a living, and for the small-holders there was the prospect of penury as described in Aristophanes' *Wealth*.

CA 39 XENOPHON, *Memorabilia* 2.7.2–6

(Aristarchus to Socrates)

2   "Since the revolution (*in 404*), there has been a mass flight to Piraeus and I have been providing a haven for the sisters, nieces and female cousins left behind – so many that we now have fourteen members of the family in the house. Our land is in the hands of the enemy, and we can get nothing from it; nor from our property, because of the depopulation of the city. No one will buy our furniture, and it is impossible to borrow money anywhere – you've as much chance of finding some in the street." . . .

3   "How is it that Ceramon, with his many dependents, manages not only to provide for himself and them, but also to put something by so as to increase his wealth, while you, with your dependents, are afraid you may all perish for want of provisions?"

4   "Simply because he has a household of slaves, and I of gentry: . . . his are workmen, mine have received a cultural education."

5   "Well now, workmen are people who make useful things – like barley-meal and bread, cloaks for men and women, short tunics, mantles and capes. You agree?"

"Certainly".

"Then does your household not know how to make any of these things?"

"On the contrary, all of them, I would say."

6   "Then don't you know that from making one of these commodities, barley-meal, Nausycides provides for himself and his household, as well as numerous pigs and cows, and even makes enough profit to be able to undertake frequent liturgies for the state; from making bread Cyrebus keeps all his family fed and maintains an opulent standard of living, while Demeas of Collytus maintains himself by making mantles, Menon from wool cloaks, and most of the Megarians from capes?"

CA 40 LYSIAS 21.11–13

(In the first ten sections of this speech (see LACTOR 5 p.50–1) the defendant describes all the liturgies he had undertaken in the previous eight years (411–403) and what they had cost him)

11   After all these risks on your behalf and these services to the city, I do not ask you, as others do, for some bounty in return, but simply ask not to be deprived of my own possessions. This would in fact be discreditable to you

12   whether I consented or not. It is not so much the prospect of the actual loss that worries me, but I am not prepared to put up with the insult nor to make it appear to those who dodge their liturgies that my expenses on your behalf are unappreciated, while their refusal to give you anything of what is theirs is approved. So if you take my advice, you will combine a

13   just verdict with respect for your own interest. You can see, gentlemen, how small the city's revenue is, and how that little is misappropriated by those in charge of it; so it is sensible to regard the property of those prepared to perform public services as the most secure form of national income.

(A similar theme is found in other speeches of Lysias; see for instance 7.31–32, 19.9–10)

CA 41 DEMOSTHENES 22.65

(An example of a farmer being unable to pay his taxes)

If he was asked which were the greater criminals against the state, thrifty farmers who because of the expense of rearing children and other private expenses or public services default on tax, or those who steal and misappropriate the money of men willing to pay tax and the money from our allies, he could scarcely have the gall to pick on those who default on contributions from their own money rather than those who steal public funds.

CA 42 ARISTOPHANES, *Wealth* 499–504

(Chremylus imagines how much better the world would be if Wealth were not blind)

CHREMYLUS. The way man's life is disposed these days, one can't help thinking that it is the work of frenzy or a malign deity. For many men who are worthless (*ponêroi*) are now wealthy from ill-gotten gains; many who are utterly worthy (*chrêstoi*) suffer misfortune and hunger.

(b) METICS AND SLAVES

1. Metics (CA 43–48)

Pericles is made to boast that Athens was one of the few Greek cities that positively welcomed foreigners (Thuc. 2.39.1). Those that did come to live in Athens as free men (metics) had certain liabilities – such as the payment of a Metic Tax, and service in the land-forces (Thuc. 2.31.2); service in the fleet was probably limited to emergencies, as in 428 (Thuc. 3.16.1); they were also expected to undertake liturgies if they could afford it. What they could not do was to achieve full citizenship except by special grant; it could not be acquired by marriage to an Athenian. They could not therefore inherit Athenian property or take any part in politics; but there was no bar on commercial activities, and some of the biggest fortunes we know about were possessed by metics.

CA 43 PLUTARCH, *Pericles* 37.2–3

In 429 Pericles was deposed from office because of opposition to his war policy, but soon reinstated.

2   When the people had apologised for their unkindness towards him, he resumed his public duties again and was elected general. He then requested the repeal of the law about illegitimate children which he himself had first introduced. This was to prevent his name and family
3   from dying out through lack of an heir. The circumstances of the law were as follows: when Pericles was at the height of his political power, many years before, and the sons he had were the legitimate ones I have mentioned (*cf. CA 134*) he introduced a law that only people born of two Athenian parents should be Athenian citizens themselves.

CA 44 XENOPHON, *Poroi (Revenues)* 2.1–2, 5

1   The metics are one of our finest resources; for not only do they maintain themselves and perform many services at no expense to the state, but they
2   also pay a Metic Tax. To show our interest in them it would be sufficient in

my opinion if we removed the disabilities which do no good to the state, but appear to detract from the status of the metics, and if we no longer
5   compelled them to serve as hoplites alongside citizens ... We would also, I think, make the metics better disposed towards us if we gave them the right to serve in the cavalry, and other attractive-looking privileges.

CA 45 ARISTOTLE, *Constitution of Athens* 58.2–3

2   Permission to bring private suits can only be obtained from the Polemarch, in cases affecting metics, including those with special tax privileges
3   (*isoteleis*), and Athenian representatives of other states (*proxenoi*). ... He himself introduces suits against metics for desertion of a patron or failure to choose one or concerning inheritances or heiresses; in other ways too the Polemarch does for metics what the Archon does for citizens.

For comment, see J. M. Moore: *Aristotle and Xenophon on Democracy and Oligarchy* pp. 297–8.

Lysias' father was a wealthy Syracusan, Cephalus, who had come to live in Piraeus in about 470. His house became a meeting-place for the sophists and their circle (see Plato *Republic* 328), but the prosperity of his business, now in the hands of his sons, attracted the rapacity of the Thirty in 404.

CA 46 LYSIAS 12.6–7

6   Theognis and Piso addressed the Thirty on the subject of metics, saying that some of them were disaffected and that this would be an excellent excuse for making some money while seeming to be punishing them; in any case, they said, the city coffers were low and the regime needed money.
7   This proposal went down well with men who thought little of murder but a great deal of making money. So they decided to arrest ten, including two paupers to mask their designs on the others with the pretence that they were acting not for money but in the interests of the community, as if their general policy had always been reasonable.

CA 47 LYSIAS 12.17–20

The Thirty gave Polemarchus their standard order to drink hemlock, without saying why he was to be put to death. So much for any
18   opportunity to stand trial and defend himself. When he was brought out dead from the prison, although we had three houses they forbade him to be carried out from any of them but hired a shack and laid him out. And although we had many burial-robes available they would not allow us to use any of them for the burial, but friends of ours severally produced a
19   robe and a pillow and other things for his burial. And although the Thirty had 700 shields of ours, and the large amount of silver and gold I have mentioned, and bronze and ornaments and furniture and female garments in a quantity beyond their dreams, and 120 slaves of which they kept the

best and gave the rest for public use, nevertheless they gave a further exhibition of their characteristic insatiable greed: Polemarchus' wife happened to be wearing gold ear-rings when Melobius first entered the house, and he took them out of her ears.

20   Their savaging of our property was ruthless. Because of our money they gave us treatment appropriate to vengeance for great crimes, though we had done nothing to deserve it from the city's point of view but had performed all our duties as *chorêgi* and paid our taxes and been well-behaved and obedient in every way, and had acquired no personal enemy but had ransomed many an Athenian from the foe. Such was the treatment they thought fit for metics who played a part in the city different from their own.

CA 48 DEMOSTHENES 36.4–6

Pasion, who died in about 370, had started life as a slave working for a banking firm. In time he rose to take over the business himself, and by his great munificence to the state won the reward of citizenship. Long after his death one of his sons brought an unsuccessful suit for 20 talents against Phormio (the "client" below) who had been made the trustee of the estate. Phormio had also been a slave originally.

4   These are the terms of the contract under which Pasion hired out his bank and his shield-factory to my client . . . but you must also learn how Pasion came to owe a further eleven talents to the bank . . .

5   Pasion had real estate worth about 20 talents and in addition more than 50 talents out on loan. Among the latter, earning interest, were 11 talents

6   from deposits in the bank. When my client hired the operation of the bank together with the deposits, realising that, if he was not yet a citizen, he would not be able to bring in all that Pasion had lent on the security of land and tenement-houses, he preferred to regard Pasion as the borrower of the 11 talents rather than the other borrowers to whom Pasion had lent them.

2. Slaves (CA 49–70)

The use of foreigners as slaves in the 5th. century was regarded as normal and morally irreproachable, so great was the prejudice against non-Greeks. In Aristotle we do at least find some questioning of the institution, though the criticisms are not very seriously entertained. The use and treatment of slaves varied greatly. They were employed widely both by the state and by the individual. Most self-employed Athenians or metics would have used slave-labour (see e.g. CA 29, 47): Thucydides (7.27.5) says that of the "more than 20,000" slaves who absconded after the Spartan occupation of Decelea in 413, the majority were artisans (*cheirotechnai*). Slaves are also found working alongside citizens at the same rates of pay on projects like the building of the Erechtheum (see CA 357). Sometimes they were given considerable responsibility and independence; but of course they were also used where working conditions were too bad for free men to endure (notably in the mines).

CA 49 XENOPHON, *Memorabilia* 2.2.2

(Socrates to Lamprocles)

"It is thought to be wrong to enslave friends, but right to enslave enemies."

CA 50 ISOCRATES 4.181

It is shameful that when in private life we regard it as right to use barbarians as slaves, in public we stand by and watch them making slaves of so many of our own allies.

CA 51 ARISTOPHANES, *Frogs* 738–753

(Xanthias, servant of Dionysus, discusses with another servant the slave-master relationship)

SERVANT. By Zeus the Saviour, your master is a gentleman.
740 XANTHIAS. He certainly is – all he knows about is swigging and frigging.
SERVANT. To think that he didn't beat you when it was clearly revealed that you, a slave, had pretended to be your master.
XANTHIAS. He would have regretted it.
SERVANT. That's proper slave talk – how I love it!
745 XANTHIAS. Excuse me – "Love it"?
SERVANT. No, I feel I'm in seventh heaven when I curse my master on the sly.
XANTHIAS. What about grumbling when you get outside the house after a beating?
SERVANT. I love that too.
XANTHIAS. And meddling?
SERVANT. Nothing like it, by Zeus.
750 XANTHIAS. Zeus of kinship, two of a kind! And overhearing the master's conversation?
SERVANT. I'm crazy about it.
XANTHIAS. What about passing it on to people outside?
SERVANT. By Zeus, when I do that it *really* switches me on.

The same situation discussed in more theoretical terms:

CA 52 ARISTOTLE, *Politics* 1253b

First let us consider master and slave, both to look at their basic relationship and also in the hopes of achieving some theoretic improvement on present conceptions. Some people think that being a master is some form of expertise, equivalent to that of running a house or running the city or running a kingdom ... Others think that being a master is contrary to nature, that although convention distinguishes between slave and free, nature knows no such distinction, and so it is not even moral, arising as it does from compulsion.

CA 53 ARISTOTLE, *Politics* 1255a

Well, it is clear that there are some who are naturally free or naturally slaves, and for such slavery is both an expedient system and a moral one. But it is not hard to see that there is something in the opposite point of view. There are two ways of interpreting the words "slavery" and "slave". There is too the legal sense of the words, where the law amounts to an agreement that the spoils of war belong to the winner. But this right many legal people accuse of violating the law, as they might a politician, regarding it as monstrous that anything won by force should be the slave and possession of him who has the power to enforce his supremacy.

Some of the occupations of state-owned slaves:

CA 54 ANDOCIDES fr. 5

Of Hyperbolus I am ashamed to speak, whose father even now is a branded slave in the public silver-mint and who himself, non-Greek foreigner that he is, makes lamps.

(*Hyperbolus was a notorious demagogue ostracised in 417 and murdered in 411; see Index*)

CA 55 ARISTOPHANES, *Lysistrata* 424–436

(*A Councillor finds the Acropolis barricaded against him by Lysistrata and the other women*)

COUNCILLOR. There's no point in just standing here. (*To his slaves, the*
425   *Scythian Archers*). Bring the crowbars so that I can put a stop to their insolence. What are you gawping at, you wretch? Looking for a drink-shop? Come on, get those crowbars up to the gates and force them apart. I'll lend a hand.
430   LYSISTRATA. Stop it; I'm coming myself. No need for crowbars. What you need is some good sense.
COUNCILLOR. Is that so, you bitch? Where's that Archer? Get hold of her and tie her hands behind her.
435   LYSISTRATA. If that public menial of yours lays the tip of a finger on me, by Artemis, he will regret it.

CA 56 ARISTOTLE, *Constitution of Athens* 54.1

Other offices elected by lot are: five road-menders whose job it is to keep the roads in repair with the assistance of state-owned workmen....

Other state-slaves included the executioner (Diodorus Siculus 13.102) and the notary (Demosthenes 19.129).

Craftsmen slaves sometimes found their own employment and simply paid a fixed amount to their masters out of their earnings.

CA 57 AESCHINES 1.97

His father left this man enough property for any other man to have been able to contribute to liturgies, but he could not even look after himself with it. He was left a house at the back of the Acropolis, a boundary estate at Sphettus and another place at Alopece; and also nine or ten house-slaves who were expert cobblers and each paid him a fee (*apophora*) of two obols a day, apart from the foreman who paid three; and furthermore a woman expert at making garments out of mallow, who took exquisite products to market, and a male embroiderer.

CA 58 ISAEUS 8.35

Ciron's property, gentlemen, consisted of an estate at Phyla worth easily as much as a talent, and two town-houses, one rented out near the temple of Dionysus in the Marshes, which would fetch 2000 dr., the other, in which he lived himself, worth 13 minas. He also had slaves out to hire and two maids and a young slave-girl and household furniture, the whole lot including the slaves being worth nearly 13 minas. So the grand total of ready capital amounted to more than 90 minas.

Female slaves were either employed domestically or in what may be loosely called "the entertainment business".

CA 59 EURIPIDES, *Trojan Women* 489–497

HECUBA. And finally, to cap all my miseries, I shall have to go to Greece in my old age as a slave woman; me, the mother of Hector, they will load with tasks most uncongenial to my years – keeping the door, guarding the keys, making the bread; and instead of a royal bed, I shall have the floor to lay my shrivelled body on, and a ragged patchwork of rags to clothe my ragged skin.

CA 60 XENOPHON, *Memorabilia* 3.11.4

Then Socrates saw that Theodote (*cf. CA 375*) was expensively got up; that her mother beside her had had an unusual amount of care expended on her clothes and appearance; that she had numerous maids who were attractive and certainly not neglected; and that no expense had been spared in fitting out her house. "Tell me, Theodote," he said, "have you got any land?"
"No."
"Well then, some property that gives you an income?"
"No."
"Well then, a workshop?"
"No."
"What do you live on then?"
"The favours of anyone willing to befriend me."

CA 61 DEMOSTHENES 59.18–19

(*The charge against Neaera was that she, a foreigner, was living with Stephanus as his wife, and trying to pass off their children as true Athenian citizens. Much is made of her past life as a slave and prostitute*)

18 (Neaera was one of) These seven young girls (who) were taken over as small children by Nicarete, a freedwoman of Charisius, the Elian, and wife of Hippias, his cook, who was clever at spotting attractive children and

19 knew how to bring them up and train them by experience, having practised the art and made her living from it. She called them her daughters, so as to extort the highest price on the grounds that they were free women from those who wanted to lie with them; but when she had exploited the youthful bloom of each, she sold off all seven of them at once as concubines.

CA 62 DEMOSTHENES 59.28–30

28 I will call Hipparchus (an Athenian) before you and compel him to give evidence or else swear on oath to his ignorance; otherwise I will serve a summons on him. Call Hipparchus.

Evidence: Hipparchus testifies that Xenoclides and he hired the defendant, Neaera, in Corinth as a concubine plying for hire, and that Neaera drank there with him and Xenoclides the poet.

29 After this she had two lovers, Timanoridas of Corinth and Eucrates of Leucas. They found Nicerate very expensive in her charges, claiming as she did to defray all her household costs at their expense; so they offered her the price of 30 minas for Neaera's body and bought Neaera from her

30 under the law of the city to be their slave once for all. They then possessed her and used her for as long as they wished. But when they were going to take a wife, they told Neaera that they did not wish to see her, their ex-concubine, plying her trade in Corinth or working for a brothel-keeper: they would rather, they said, accept a smaller sum from her than they had paid for her and see her lot improved. So they remitted the sum of 1,000 dr. (500 dr. each) for her to buy her freedom, and told her to pay them the remaining 20 minas, when she could.

The treatment of slaves:

CA 63 XENOPHON, *Economicus* 3.4

(*Socrates to Critobulus*)

"Again, if I showed you how in some places nearly all the slaves are in chains, but still frequently run away, and in others they are unconfined, but are willing to stay and work, wouldn't this also appear to be a significant factor in estate-management?"

CA 64 XENOPHON, *Economicus* 9.5

(*Among the things on his estate which Ischomachus shows his wife*)

"I showed her also the women's quarters which were separated from the men's by a bolted door, to prevent any undesirable traffic between the two, and to stop the slaves breeding without our consent. For if good slaves are allowed to breed, it usually makes them amenable, but if bad ones are paired, they are even more productive of trouble."

CA 65 XENOPHON, *Memorabilia* 2.1.16–17

(*Socrates to Aristippus*)

16 "But let us also consider how their masters treat such lazy slaves. Do they not curb their lubricity by starvation, and prevent them from stealing by keeping their goods locked up? Do they not put them in chains to stop

them running away, and flog them to keep them from idleness? Or do you treat such slaves any differently?"

17   "I use every kind of punishment to reduce them to submission."

The economics of slavery:

CA 66 ML 79.33–46

(*Sale of confiscated property belonging to the mutilators of the Hermae, 414*)

The property of Cephisodorus, (metic) living in Peiraeus:

Slaves: Thracian female, 165dr; Thracian female, 135dr; Thracian male, 170dr; Syrian male, 240dr; Carian male, 105dr; Illyrian male, 161dr; Thracian female, 220dr; Thracian male, 115dr; . . . Carian boy 174dr; little Carian boy 72dr.

(*The normal daily wage at this period was 1 drachma, which would be just enough to feed a small family*)

For slaves with management responsibilities higher prices could be expected.

CA 67 XENOPHON, *Economicus* 12.3–4

3   Socrates said: "Tell me, Ischomachus, when you need an estate-manager, do you look round to find a man with experience of management, and then try and buy him . . . or do you train him in management yourself?"

4   "Most certainly I try to do the training myself."

CA 68 XENOPHON, *Memorabilia* 2.5.2

Socrates to Antisthenes, on the value of friendship.

"One slave might be worth two minas, another not even half a mina, another five, another as much as ten; and Nicias son of Niceratus is said to have paid a talent for a manager of his silver-mines."

CA 69 XENOPHON, *Poroi (Revenues)* 4.14

Those of us who have given thought to the matter have heard long ago that Nicias the son of Niceratus once owned a thousand slaves in the silver mines, and these he hired out to Sosias the Thracian on condition that Sosias paid each slave an obol a day nett, and always kept their number the same.

CA 70 XENOPHON, *Poroi (Revenues)* 4.22,25

22   Perhaps someone is wondering how, when there are plenty of workmen, a lot of people will also be found who are ready to hire them; then let him take heart when he notices that many people who are well supplied will hire the public slaves in addition (for they have abundant resources); and there are many of these labourers too who are growing old on the job, and many others, both Athenians and foreigners, who would not be able to do physical work and would not wish to either, but would gladly earn their living by using their intelligence as overseers.

   Xenophon calculates that the state could own 10,000 slaves, bringing in an annual revenue of 100 talents.

25   I could produce evidence that the city will receive many times more than this sum, if there are people still alive who remember how much the duty on prisoners-of-war was bringing in before the events at Decelea. And there is other evidence of this too, namely that although countless slaves have worked in the silver-mines throughout history, yet the mines are now no different from what our ancestors remembered them to be.

(c) THE FAMILY

1. Citizenship and Inheritance (CA 71–79)

For detailed treatment of all the topics introduced in the rest of this chapter, see especially W. K. Lacey: *The Family in Classical Greece*, ch.IV-VII.

The Athenian laws of citizenship and inheritance were intended to keep the household (*oikos*) together as a unit, and to prevent its dilution either by the admixture of non-Athenian blood, or by its transference to a non-blood relation. Sons inherited as a matter of course, and a man could divide his estate between any number of them, thus creating new *oikoi*; but if he only had daughters to inherit, they were termed *epiklêroi* and became the responsibility of their male next of kin, who might either marry them in person or arrange for their marriage to someone else. The inheritance was held in trust for their children.

CA 71 DEMOSTHENES 43.19

Buselus of the deme of Oeum had five sons . . . who all grew to manhood, and Buselus shared his estate rightly and fairly among them. Taking their share each married a wife in accordance with Athenian law and they all had children and grandchildren, and from the single original household of Buselus there sprang five new households, each son living separately with his own house and his own children.

The order of inheritance:

CA 72 ISAEUS 11.1–3

1   I have read you the laws because he falsely claims that according to the first of them the child has a right to half the inheritance. Hagnias was not our brother, but in the case of a brother's money the law lays down that the right to inherit goes first to brothers and their sons, provided the
2   brothers come from the same father, these being the next-of-kin: if they do not exist, the next in line are sisters from the same father and their children: if these do not exist, the third in line are cousins on the father's side and cousins' children. If none of these survive, then the right reverts to the mother's side and the order of precedence is as for the father's side.
3   These are the only claims the law-giver admits – more briefly than I have stated them, but his intention is clearly as I have described.

The assignment of heiresses (*epiklêroi*) to guardians (*kyrioi*):

CA 73 DEMOSTHENES 46.22–23

22   The Law decrees that there must be a legal assignment of all heiresses, foreign or Athenian, the Archon being responsible for bringing cases

non-Athenian — citizen — not — slave

concerning citizens, the Polemarch for metics, and that no-one can have an inheritance or an heiress without such legal assignment.

(The Law is then quoted)

23 My opponent should have taken his claim for the heiress, whether based on right through gift or on right through kindred, before the appropriate Archon, and have convinced a panel of jurors and gained a verdict in a legal fashion.

CA 74 PLUTARCH, *Solon* 20.2

There may perhaps be something absurd and ridiculous about the law which entitles an heiress to marry one of her husband's closest relations if he himself, her lawful lord and master, proves impotent. Some however say that this is a good way of dealing with men who are incapable of intercourse, but marry heiresses for their money, and do violence to nature under cover of the law.

An instance of the strength of family feeling:

CA 75 ANDOCIDES 1.117–120

117 Epilycus was my uncle on my mother's side. He died in Sicily leaving no
118 sons but two daughters, who passed to me and Leagrus. The family finances were in a bad way, since Epilycus' ready estate amounted to less than two talents, though outstanding debts came to more than five. All the same I summoned Leagrus and before the witness of friends said that it
119 was our duty in these circumstances to prove our family feeling. "It is not right" I said "for us to claim money belonging to others or a prosperous marriage, and to scorn Epilycus' daughters. Had Epilycus been alive or had he died and left a lot of money, as next of kin we should
120 have claimed the girls as a right . . .; as things are we must have them as a duty. So you claim legal rights to one, and I will claim rights to the other." He agreed and we acted accordingly.

The acquisition of an heiress to look after could entitle a man to dissolve his current marriage.

CA 76 DEMOSTHENES 57.40–41

40 My mother gave birth first to a daughter by Protomachus, to whom her brother by the same father and mother had given her: then by my father she gave birth to me. I will now tell you how she came to live with my
41 father. . . . Protomachus was poor: he inherited an heiress of comfortable means and wanting to give away my mother he persuaded my father Thucritus, an acquaintance of his, to take her. My father had my mother betrothed to him by her brother Timocrates, and the betrothal was witnessed by both his uncles and by others.

The problems of female inheritance could be avoided by adopting a male heir.

CA 77 DEMOSTHENES 41.3

Polyeuctus was from Teithras; . . . not having any male issue, he adopted Leocrates his wife's brother. He had two daughters by Leocrates' sister, the elder of whom he gave to me with a dowry of 40 minas and the younger to Leocrates.

CA 78 ISAEUS 2.13–14, 18

13   I will show that my adoption was legal. Read the law which lays down that a man may dispose of his property as he wishes, provided he has no true-born male children. . . . The law-giver made the law because he saw that the only refuge and solace for childless people in their lonely life is the
14   right to adopt whom they wish. Such being the law on adoption, and he being childless, Menecles adopted me, not in his will at the point of death, as often happens, nor at a time of illness; but in good health, advisedly and in his right mind, he adopted me and introduced me to his clansmen in the presence of these gentlemen and enrolled me among his demesmen and
18   the *orgeônes* (*a religious organisation*). Then Menecles began to look out for a wife for me and said I should marry; and I took the daughter of Philonides. Menecles was showing the forethought you would expect a father to show for his son, and I in turn attended to him and respected him as if he were my natural father, and so did my wife, so that he sang our praises to all his demesmen.

The rights of citizenship were jealously guarded (see CA 43), and the conduct of Neaera could be represented as a threat to the integrity of the Athenian family (see CA 61–62).

CA 79 DEMOSTHENES 59.112–113

112   (If the case goes against us . . .) prostitutes will have absolute licence to live with whoever they want and to say their children come from any father they pick on. . . . And look at it from the point of view of female citizens
113   and the risk to the daughters of poor men of becoming indisposable. As things are, even if a woman has no means, the law grants her an adequate dowry, if she is at all reasonably good-looking; but if the law is trampled in the dust in this case . . ., prostitution will be the fate of female citizens if they are indisposable through poverty, and the status of free women will pass to concubines, if they can freely bear children at will and take part in the various rites of the city.

2. Betrothal and Marriage (CA 80–103)

Formal betrothal was usually regarded as a necessary preliminary to marriage. It was a matter for the girl's father or guardian – with or without the help of professional match-makers – to arrange with the prospective bridegroom; oaths were exchanged in the presence of witnesses, and a dowry agreed. This might be done many years before the wedding itself could take place, as in the case of Demosthenes' sister. Only in unusual circumstances did the girl have any choice of husband. Guardians however took their responsibilities seriously, and the provision of a dowry was a matter of pride; relations, or even occasionally the state, might make contributions towards it, rather than leave a girl undowered. Prospects for the girl without a dowry were poor unless a particularly generous husband could be found prepared to go without it.

Marriage was seen principally as an institution for raising legitimate children and maintaining the home. A marriage without children could well give rise to divorce – which could be instituted by either wife or husband; in each case the dowry had to be returned.

The Athenian attitude to adultery was largely determined by the importance attached to legitimate succession. A child born of a mixed marriage between Athenian and non-Athenian, or of a liaison between a married Athenian and an Athenian woman other than his wife, would have no claim to inheritance or kinship, and would be excluded from the important religious observances of the family. Strong pressure was therefore applied to discourage such unions. The statutory penalties for adultery were death for the man and divorce for the woman, though this cannot have been the invariable practice (especially where large dowries were concerned), and Comedy offers us some colourful alternatives.

CA 80 DEMOSTHENES 46.18

(*Quotation of Law*)

The children of a woman whom her father or brother from the same father or grandfather on the father's side has legally betrothed shall be deemed true-born. But if the woman has no such relations alive if she is an heiress, her guardian shall have her; if she is not, she can give herself to anyone as guardian.

CA 81 XENOPHON, *Memorabilia* 2.6.36

(*Socrates to Critobulus*)

"Aspasia used to say that good match-makers showed their skill in bringing people together by passing good and truthful reports between them; deception she had nothing to say for, since people who are deceived take as much dislike for the match-maker as they do for each other."

CA 82 DEMOSTHENES 27.4–5, 17

4   Demosthenes, my father, left behind him an estate worth nearly fourteen talents, myself aged seven, my sister aged five, and our mother who had contributed 50 minas to the family finances. Planning on the point of death for our futures, he put everything in the hands of Aphobus here and Demophon, both nephews of his, . . . and of Therippides of our deme, no
5   relation but a boyhood friend. To Therippides he gave seventy minas from my share of the inheritance for him to enjoy the interest until I came of age, in the hope that this would prevent his mishandling my affairs through greed for money. To Demophon he gave my sister and two talents for his immediate possession. To Aphobus here he gave my mother, eighty minas as a dowry, the house to live in and my furniture to use. He supposed that if he thus bound these men to me by closer family ties he would make them better guardians. . . .
17   . . . In the event of Aphobus' not marrying my mother, the law states that he owes the dowry plus 18% interest: but I am calculating at 12% only

and on this basis capital and interest for ten years add up to about 3 talents.

CA 83 DEMOSTHENES 27.69

My father would be greatly distressed if he knew that I, his son, risked having to pay the fine of $\frac{1}{6}$ on the dowries and legacies which he himself had given to the defendants, and that whereas other guardians had often provided at their own expense for the marriage of the daughters of needy friends as well as needy relations, Aphobus refused even to give back his dowry, and that ten years after receiving it.

CA 84 PLUTARCH, *Cimon* 4.7

There are some who say that Elpinice lived with Cimon (*her brother*) without any concealment, in a state of evident matrimony, since her poverty prevented her obtaining a husband to match her noble birth; but when Callias, a prosperous Athenian, fell in love with her and showed himself ready to pay into the Treasury the fine imposed on her father, she gave her consent, and Cimon presented her to Callias.

CA 85 ISAEUS 1.39

If Polyarchus, Cleonymus' father and our grandfather, were alive and lacking the necessities of life, or if Cleonymus had died leaving daughters in need, we because of our relationship (*i.e. as Cleonymus' nephews*) would have had to look after our grandfather in his old age and either ourselves take Cleonymus' daughters to wife or provide dowries and give them away. Our kinship and the laws and our respect for you would compel this, the alternative being severe penalties, and deep disgrace.

CA 86 DEMOSTHENES 43.54

(*Quotation of Law*)

When a female assessed as a Thete has a right of inheritance, if the nearest relation in her family does not wish to marry her, he shall give her away from the family, adding to any property of her own a dowry of 500dr. if he is a Pentecosiomedimnus, 300dr. if a Knight, and 150dr. if a Zeugites. Where there are several relatives in the same relationship to her, they shall make proportionate contributions to the dowry.

CA 87 PLUTARCH, *Aristides* 27.1, 3–4

1   It is recorded that Aristides' daughters were given in marriage from the Prytaneum at public expense, with the state acting as the brides' father, and voting 3000 drachmas to each as dowry; also that his son Lysimachus was given 100 minas of silver, and 100 *plethra* of farming land by the state, as well as a daily allowance of four drachmas, under a law proposed by Alcibiades....

3   Demetrius of Phalerum asserts in his *Socrates* that he remembers that Lysimachus, the grandson of Aristides (*his daughter's son*), used to earn a living as a very young man from a tablet containing interpretations of

dreams, as he sat beside the so-called Iacchium. Demetrius introduced a proposal and persuaded the people to give to Lysimachus' mother and
4 sister three obols a day for their keep. It is not at all surprising that the state took such care of people in the city; for when they learned that a granddaughter of Aristogeiton was living humbly in Lemnos, unable to get a husband because of her poverty, they brought her back to Athens, gave her a well-born husband, and presented her with the estate of Potamus by way of a dowry.

CA 88 DEMOSTHENES 59.8

It seemed unlikely he would be able to give away his other daughter: for who would have taken her without a dowry from an impoverished father, owing money to the Treasury?

(*The person here referred to is Apollodorus, threatened with ruination by Neaera's husband*)

CA 89 SOPHOCLES, *Oedipus Tyrannus* 1492–1502

OEDIPUS (*to his infant children after blinding himself*): But when you come to the age of marriage, who could there be who would take the risk of incurring the shame and reproaches which will fall to my daughters and to them besides?... Who will marry you? No-one, my children. Without doubt you will have to end your lives unwed and barren.

CA90 LYSIAS 19.14–15

14 (My father) when he was of marrying age and he could have married someone else who would have brought a large sum of money with her, (he) married my mother who brought nothing; he did so because she was the daughter of Xenophon, Euripides' son, who not only seemed a good man
15 in himself but had also, I hear, been elected general by you. As for my sisters, though some quite rich men were willing to take them without a dowry, he did not bestow them on these suitors as being, he thought, of inferior birth, but one he bestowed on Philomelus of the Paeanian deme, generally regarded as well-born rather than rich, and the other on a man blamelessly poor, and his two nieces on Phaedrus of the Myrrhinusian deme with a dowry of 40 minas and on Aristophanes with a similar dowry.

(*The speaker is not identified*)

CA 91 XENOPHON, *Memorabilia* 2.2.4

(*Socrates to Lamprocles*)

"You surely don't suppose that it is sexual desire alone which leads men to beget children, when the streets and the brothels afford ample opportunities for gratifying that. It is clear that we consider what sort of women would give us the best children, and then unite with them to produce children.''

CA 92 DEMOSTHENES 59.122

Living together means producing children, enrolling sons among clansmen and demesmen and giving away daughters as one's own to husbands. Courtesans we have for pleasure and concubines to satisfy our daily bodily needs, but wives to produce true-born children and to be trustworthy guardians of the household.

CA 93 DEMOSTHENES 59.81–82

81   When the Areopagus took a grave view of the matter and wanted to punish Theogenes (*Archon at the time*) for taking an unsuitable wife and allowing her to conduct sacred and secret rites on behalf of the city, Theogenes implored them for mercy, saying that he did not know she was Neaera's daughter but had been cheated by Stephanus and had supposed he was marrying Stephanus' own true-born daughter in a properly legal manner; and that it was his inexperience and *naïveté* that had made him take Stephanus as his assessor to help him in his office as a supposed friend
82   and this was the reason he had married, as he thought, into his family. ''As proof of this . . .'' he said ''I will dismiss the woman from my house.''

CA 94 ISAEUS 2.6–9

6   After giving away our sisters, being ourselves of military age we went abroad on campaign in Thrace with Iphicrates: after acquiring a bit of capital there which improved our credit, we returned to Athens and found that our elder sister now had two children but the younger, Menecles'
7   wife, was childless. One or two months later Menecles, after singing our sister's praises, made proposals to us, saying that he mistrusted his own age and childlessness and that she deserved a better reward for her goodness than to grow old with him without a child: his own misfortune
8   was enough. He asked us to please him by giving her, with his approval, to another man. We said he must get her approval: we would do whatever
9   she thought best. At first she would not even listen to the suggestion, but in time she reluctantly gave way. This is how we came to give her to Elius of Sphettus, and Menecles gave her back her dowry . . . and the dresses she had when she came to him and the bits of gold she possessed.

CA 95 DEMOSTHENES 30.8

(*When Demosthenes won the case against his former guardian Aphobus, he was still unable to collect the sum owing to him, as the farm of which he tried to take possession was now in the hands of Onetor, whose sister Aphobus had married*)

When Aphobus lost the guardianship case, he still had no wish to act properly, and Onetor didn't even try to settle the matter: he said that he had given his sister a dowry – though in fact he hadn't at all, but was still in possession of it – but that she had divorced her husband, and he had been unable to recover it, so he had mortgaged the farm, and now had the cheek to turn me off it.

The Athenians seem to have shared the traditional prejudice against stepmothers.

CA 96 EURIPIDES, *Alcestis* 304–310

(*Alcestis, before her death, asks her husband Admetus to care for the children*)

Keep those children as masters of my house, and do not marry again – for a stepmother who was less noble than I would come down heavily on our children from jealousy. Do not do this I beg you. For a stepmother who is ill-disposed toward the children is as vicious as a viper.

CA 97 DEMOSTHENES 59.16

(*Quotation of Law*)

If an alien man cohabits with a female citizen in any way whatsoever, anyone who wishes and has the right shall indict him before the *Thesmothetae*. If he is convicted, he and his property shall be sold, and one third given to the successful prosecutor. The same procedure shall be followed if an alien woman lives with a male citizen; if she is convicted, he shall be fined 1000 dr.

CA 98 LYSIAS 1.30–33

(*The speaker here is Euphiletus; he was being prosecuted for killing Eratosthenes whom he had caught in the act of adultery with his wife*)

30 You have just heard, gentlemen, that the court of the Areopagus itself, which traditionally and in our own time has been assigned the task of judging cases of murder, has been explicitly instructed that a man should not be found guilty of murder who finds an adulterer with his wife and
31 exacts vengeance. So convinced was the lawgiver of the rightness of this attitude to wedded wives, that he extended the law to apply to courtesans too, inferior in status though they are. Yet it is obvious that, had he been able to think of a severer penalty in the case of wedded wives, he would have decreed it. As it was, he couldn't. Hence the equal treatment of wives and courtesans. Read me the law . . .
32 You hear, gentlemen, that the law ordains that if someone brings shame on a free man or child by force, he must pay twofold recompense; but if he brings shame on a woman, he comes in the category where killing is permitted. So you see the law regards violation as deserving a lighter penalty than seduction: for the latter it decrees death, for the former
33 double recompense, the theory being that those who work their will by violence are hated by those they violate, whereas those who seduce so corrupt the women's souls that they make other people's wives closer to themselves than to their rightful husbands, and establish an influence on

the whole household by confusing the issue between husband's children and adulterer's.

CA 99 DEMOSTHENES 59.86–87

86   The only women forbidden by law to attend public rites are those found with an adulterer: if such a woman does so attend illegally, anyone is free without penalty to inflict any punishment on her, apart from death . . . The purpose of the law is to prevent pollution and desecration of the rites by setting up an adequate deterrent to wives which will ensure their rectitude as upright keepers of the home, on penalty of dismissal from their husband's house and from all public rites . . .

87   (*Law on Adultery*)
"When a man catches an adulterer, he shall not continue to live with his wife; if he does, he shall forfeit citizen rights . . ." (*The law continues as above*).
      (*The penalties are set out more explicitly in CA 117*)

CA 100 DEMOSTHENES 23.53

(*Quotation of Law*)

If someone kills another at a sports contest unintentionally or in a road accident, or in a war by mistake, or in protecting his wife or mother or sister or daughter or concubine, provided she can legally bear him free children, the killer shall not be liable to exile.

CA 101 ANDOCIDES 4.13–14

13   I am amazed at those who think Alcibiades is a democrat – and fail to turn their eyes to the selfish arrogance of his private life. He married Callias' sister receiving a dowry of ten talents; then when Hipponicus was killed in action as general at Delium he extorted a further ten talents, claiming that Hipponicus had said he would add another ten when his daughter gave
14   birth. Then after thus receiving a dowry of unprecedented size, he had the insolence to bring into the same household courtesans, free and slave, thus forcing his wife, a decent woman, to desert him, after first going to the archon as the law enjoins.

CA 102 ARISTOHANES, *Clouds* 1071–1085

(*Phidippides is undergoing instruction*)

UNJUST ARGUMENT. Young man, consider everything that self-control has to offer, then think of all the pleasures you would be depriving yourself of – boys, women, party-games ('*cottabos*', *cf. CA 479*), food and drink
1075   and laughter. Is life even worth living without all those? Well, next I'll go on to the urgings of nature. You fall: lust; a spot of adultery; then you get caught. You've had it, because you can't talk your way out. But stick with me, and you can follow your urges, frolic, laugh, and think nothing immoral. If you get caught in adultery, your plea will be that
1080   you did nothing wrong. Then blame it on Zeus, who also succumbed to lust and women; you're only a mortal, so how could you do better than a god?

> JUST ARGUMENT. But if he listens to you, and then gets the radish and ember treatment, how can he argue his way out of being called a bugger?
>
> UNJUST ARGUMENT. What's wrong with being called a bugger?
>
> (*For 'the radish and ember treatment' see Dover, Aristophanes, Clouds (OUP 1970), note on lines 981, 1083*).

In the last decade of the Peloponnesian War the normal law of legitimacy was put in temporary abeyance.

CA 103 DIOGENES LAERTIUS 2.26

> It is said that when the Athenians wanted to increase the population because of shortage of manpower they passed a decree that one could marry one citizen but beget children also by a second. Hence Socrates did this.

3. HOMOSEXUALITY (CA 104–111)

Homosexual attachments had long been an accepted part of Athenian life (see for instance the story of Harmodius and Aristogiton in Thuc.6.54ff.); but this does not mean that they were indiscriminately pursued. There was legislation against procuring for boys, and against homosexual relations between adults. The evidence of Plato and of vases (see e.g. Pl.17 in Lacey) suggests that boys might expect to receive such attention only for a few years after entering puberty, and that their lovers would only have been a little bit older. Even then it seems to have been limited mainly to the upper class, perhaps on grounds of expense. There is little reason for supposing that it interfered with the development of heterosexual relations, particularly as men might expect not to marry until they were over 30 (30–35 is the age approved in Plato *Laws* 721b).

CA 104 AESCHINES 1.13, 18–20

13   The law explicitly states that if a father or brother or uncle or guardian or in short any person responsible hires out a boy to be a sexual companion, the boy himself shall not be liable to public prosecution but the person who hired him out and the person who paid for his services . . .; the law lays down equal penalties for each, adding that the boy is under no compulsion when he comes to manhood to keep his father or provide him with a house, though he must bury him and carry out the customary rites

18   when he dies. Once the boy is enrolled in the deme roll and knows and understands the city's laws and can distinguish between right and wrong,

19   then the law speaks directly to him, saying that if any Athenian becomes a sexual companion he shall not become one of the nine archons, . . . nor hold any sacred office, being a person of impure body let alone mind, nor take the part of a public advocate nor hold any office at any time at home

20   or abroad, whether awarded by lot or by vote; nor shall he be a herald or an ambassador nor pass judgement on ex-ambassadors, nor give information against anyone for money, nor speak in the *Boulê* or the Assembly,

however good a speaker he is. The law makes any offender liable to public prosecution and lays down the sternest penalties.

CA 105 PLATO, *Symposium* 181a–e

(*The speaker is Pausanias*)

The love associated with Aphrodite Pandemus is, as the name implies, a

b vulgar love and operates in an indiscriminate way: this is the love practised by inferior mortals. Such men in the first place love women as much as boys; secondly where they love, they love the body rather than the mind; thirdly they choose as objects of their love the most unintelligent they can find, their eyes solely on the objective and not on the quality of their love. So their behaviour is indiscriminate, sometimes good, sometimes the opposite. For this love comes both from much the younger of the two

c Aphrodites and from the one in whose birth male and female were concerned. On the other hand the love associated with Aphrodite Urania works for a goddess who, first, had her birth from a male origin only – hence the love of boys – and secondly is older and free from violent instincts. Thus those who feel the breath of this love turn to the male, finding satisfaction in what is naturally stronger and more intelligent; and even in the love of boys, those purely inspired by this sort of love are easily

d recognisable, since their love is not for young boys but for boys whose intelligence is maturing, that is about the time of their first growth of beard. I think those who begin their love at that point are prepared for a lifetime association and companionship and are not prepared to trick their victim, catching him young and foolish, and then to run off after someone else with a cynical jeer. Actually there ought to have been a law against

e loving young boys, to avoid much expenditure of energy on uncertain ends, since the outcome of such love and its effect for good or ill on mind and body is unpredictable. Good men impose this discipline on themselves, but we ought to compel the ordinary lover too to adopt it, just as we compel him, as far as we can, not to have *affaires* with free women.

CA 106 PLUTARCH, *Alcibiades* 4.1, 3–4

1 Many of the nobility pressed their company and their attention upon him; some of them were clearly captivated, bowled over by his extraordinary beauty; but the love which Socrates felt for him was plain proof of the

3 boy's natural goodness ... As he got used to Socrates, and listened to the words of a lover who was not in quest of unmanly pleasures, and not even trying to kiss and fondle him, but whose aim was to correct the bad part of his nature and deflate his empty and foolish affectations, he cowered like a

4 beaten cock that trails its feathers ... In the end everyone was amazed to see him sharing his meals, his exercise, and his tent with Socrates, while to his other lovers he showed himself unapproachable and hard to get.

CA 107 PLATO, *Symposium* 217a–d, 218b–d

(*The speaker is Alcibiades*)

Supposing that he was attracted by my youthful beauty I thought this a wonderful piece of luck which would enable me by pleasing Socrates to hear all that he knew; for I thought very highly of my good looks. With this in mind, I dismissed the attendant who had always previously

b accompanied me on visits to Socrates and began to visit him – the truth must out – alone. But mark this, – and correct me if I lie, Socrates, – we were alone together and I expected him to utter to me the sort of things a lover says to his boyfriend in solitude, and I was agog. But none of this happened: he just spoke to me and spent the day with me in the usual way

c and pushed off. Next I urged him to take exercise with me, and I set about it hoping to achieve something by this means. Well, he exercised with me and wrestled often with me when no one else was present. But – need you ask? – I got nowhere. Foiled in this attempt, I decided I must keep up the pressure and not let up having once put my hand to the task, but really find out the truth of the matter. So I asked him to dinner, just like a lover

d scheming to get his boyfriend. He wasn't quick in accepting this invitation either, but eventually he complied. The first time he came, he wanted to depart immediately after dinner and I hadn't the nerve to stop him. Then I schemed again and this time after dinner I kept on conversing far into the night; and when he wanted to depart, on the grounds that it was late, I made him stay. So he reposed on the couch next to mine, the one on which he had dined, and there was no one else sleeping in the room, just

218b ourselves. . . . When the lamp was put out and the slaves were outside, I

c decided not to beat about the bush with him but come out into the open with my thoughts, and I nudged him and said "Are you asleep, Socrates?" "No" he said. "I've come to a conclusion" I said. "What conclusion?" "I think" I said "that you are the only worthy lover I have had and that you are shy of mentioning the fact to me. My own attitude is this. I think it

d would be downright stupid not to grant you this request and any other demand you may have on my property or my friends. For me there is nothing more important than improving myself to the maximum, and I think no one will help me more in this than you. If I refused to gratify a man like you I should feel much more shame before the wise than I would before the vulgar herd if I gratified him."

CA 108 XENOPHON, *Symposium* 4.15

(*Critobulus is explaining why he is proud of his beauty*).

"You, Callias, make much of your ability to improve people's sense of right; but I think I have a better right than you to say that I lead men on to every kind of virtue. Handsome fellows like us provide the sort of inspiration which makes our lovers more open-handed with their money, more conscientious and ambitious for honour in time of danger, and even more modest and self-controlled, in that they have inhibitions about what they most want."

CA 109 XENOPHON. *Memorabilia* 1.3.11

(*Socrates criticises Critobulus for daring to kiss Alcibiades' handsome son*)

"You poor fellow" said Socrates. "What do you think will become of you after kissing a handsome boy? You will lose your freedom and become a slave, you will spend lavishly on pleasures that do you no good, you will have no time for cultivating the pursuits of a gentleman, but will be compelled to devote yourself to things that even a madman would have no time for."

(*cf. CA 27*)

The Sausage-seller's passion for Demos raises him to the level of the "good men and true", i.e. the Knights (cf. CA 38).

CA 110 ARISTOPHANES, *Knights* 730–740

(*Demos is disturbed by a racket outside his house, and comes out to find what the trouble is*)

730   DEMOS. What's the matter with you, Paphlagon?
     CLEON. For your sake I'm being beaten up by this chap and his young
       men.
     DEMOS. Why?
     CLEON. Because I love and adore you, Demos.
     DEMOS. And who are *you*?
     SAUSAGE-SELLER. I am his rival; I have long been in love with you and
735   wanted to serve you – so do many good men and true. But we can't
      because of him. And you are just like all the boys one falls in love with.
      You won't receive the good men and true, but give yourself to the
740   sellers of lamps and leather, the stitchers and cobblers of shoes.

An older man's love for a young boy was regarded as ridiculous, even if in this case not illegal as the boy was a slave.

CA 111 LYSIAS 3.4–5

4   If I am in the wrong, Councillors, I do not ask for pardon: but if I prove that in this matter I am not guilty of what Simon has sworn to but have merely shown myself rather foolish for my age in my attitude to the young lad, then I ask you to think none the worse of me, realising that all men are naturally desirous and that respectability lies in handling these desires as decorously as possible. In this Simon has constantly obstructed me, as I shall show.

5   We were both smitten with Theodotus, this young lad from Plataea. I wanted to make him my friend by kindnesses, but Simon wanted to force him to do what he wanted by unscrupulous violence. What Theodotus suffered from Simon would fill a book: what I suffered I want to tell you.

4. The Role of Women (CA 112–141)

Pericles' dictum (Thuc.2.45.2) that the best women were those who attracted least attention from men, suggests that they were little more than doormats. And there is plenty of evidence to support this view: the legal and political disabilities they suffered, the restrictions on their movements and activities, the suspicion of the educated female, and the chauvinistic behaviour of some husbands. This however gives a very one-sided picture. The only really independent women in Athens may have been those like Aspasia whose foreign nationality freed them from many conventional restraints; similar non-Athenian women also figure prominently in the drama; but even among citizens we can find instances of female dominance, quite apart from the three great feminist fantasies of Aristophanes – *Lysistrata, Thesmophoriazusae* and *Ecclesiazusae*. In this, as in other social matters, the Peloponnesian War probably had a liberating effect, not least because it reduced social convention: they simply had to work, making things and selling them in the open market, in order to support their families.

Legal disabilities on women:

CA 112 ISAEUS 10.10

The law expressly says that no child or woman shall have the power to make any contract above the value of a medimnus of barley.

The law did not however prevent all financial transactions with women.

CA 113 DEMOSTHENES 41.8–9

8   Aristogenes testified that Polyeuctus on his death-bed claimed that two minas were owed to him, which Spudias had, together with the interest – this was the price of a house-slave, which Spudias had bought from Polyeuctus; but he neither paid the price at the time nor has he now brought it into account – and also 1,800 drachmas. I can't think how

9   Spudias will excuse the latter defalcation, for he borrowed the money from Polyeuctus' wife and she left written evidence of this at her death and her brothers witnessed the whole transaction and inquired into the details to prevent any unpleasantness between us.

CA 114 DEMOSTHENES 43.62

(Quotation of Law of Solon)

(The person responsible) shall lay out the corpse inside the house, as he thinks fit. He shall carry out the corpse on the following day before sunrise. The men shall walk in front in the burial procession, the women behind. No woman under sixty years of age, apart from relatives down to and including cousins, shall enter the laying-out room, nor follow the corpse to the cemetery.

CA 115 DEMOSTHENES 46.14

(Quotation of Law)

Any man ... shall be permitted to dispose of his estate as he wishes, provided he has no true-born male issue, and provided madness or senility or drugs or disease or a woman's persuasion have not disturbed his judgement and he has not been under compulsion or duress.

CA 116 DEMOSTHENES 43.51

(Quotation of Law)

If a man dies intestate and without sons, his property shall pass to the following, as well as (if they exist) to any surviving daughters. First to brothers from the same father, second to true-born sons of such brothers; if these do not exist, to their sons. Male issue and relationship to the father shall prevail, even if the relationship is more remote, as far as cousins: but if there are no male cousins on the father's side, males on the mother's side shall inherit on the same principles. If no male relation survives under any of these heads, the nearest surviving relation on the father's side shall inherit. No bastard, male or female, shall have rights of inheritance. Dated from the archonship of Euclides (*403*).

CA 117 AESCHINES 1.183

Solon, our most famous law-giver, drafted a law with true ancient solemnity about the decency of wives, forbidding any wife taken in adultery to adorn herself or attend any public sacred ceremony, lest by mixing with guiltless wives she should corrupt them; if she does attend or adorn herself, Solon bids anyone witnessing it to tear her garments and strip her of her finery and beat her, stopping short of killing her or maiming her: thus does Solon seek to disgrace such a wife and make her life unbearable. (*See CA 99*)

Some differing views of the character and status of women:

CA 118 PLATO, *Laws* 780d–781b

e   Your arrangements, Clinias (*Cretan*) and Megillus (*Spartan*), for men to feed together are excellent . . ., but quite wrongly the women have been left

781 to their own devices uncontrolled by law and their manner of feeding together has not been brought into the open, but the naturally more secretive and furtive human sex has, because of its weakness, wrongly been left by an indulgent law-giver in a state of disorder. This laxity has resulted in many things going wrong which would have been much better for the control of law; for this casual neglect of women does not just amount, as you might think, to a neglect of half the whole problem – it

b   amounts to a neglect of more than half to the extent that a woman's natural capacity for virtue is less than a man's.

CA 119 ARISTOPHANES, *Lysistrata* 7–19

CALONICE. What is troubling you? Do not scowl, child. It doesn't suit you to shoot your brows together.

9   LYSISTRATA. My heart is on fire, Calonice, and it makes me cross that though we women are regarded among men as mischief-makers. . .
CALONICE. And so we are . . .
LYSISTRATA. Yet when they are told to meet here to make plans about a

15   very important matter, they are still asleep; they haven't come.
CALONICE. They will come, my dear. You know how hard it is for women to get out; one of us is pottering around her husband, another rousing a slave; then there are the children to be put to bed, and washed and fed.

CA 120 ARISTOPHANES, *Thesmophoriazusae* 786–800, 830–842

(*The women of the Chorus speak in the Parabasis*)

Everyone has got lots of bad things to say about women, how we are a bad influence on men, and responsible for conflicts, quarrels, faction, trouble, anguish, war – the lot. Well, if we're a bad lot, really and truly, why do you

790 marry us, and forbid us to leave the house, or even to be seen peeping outside? Do you really mean to keep such a close eye on a bad lot? . . . And

795 if we spend the night at someone else's house, having a bit of fun and

wearing ourselves out everyone comes snooping round the couches looking for this bad lot. And if she peeps out of a window, you want to get a look at her; and if she retreats in shame, everyone is all the keener to see

800 the bad lot peeping out again. So we are quite clearly a much better lot than you, and the evidence is right in front of you ... (*There follows a series of unfavourable comparisons between individual men of public note,*

830 *and women*) ... There are plenty of charges that we women could hold against men, but this is the biggest. If one of us gives birth to a man who does his city good, like a captain or a general, she ought to get some

835 honour, a front seat at the Stenia and the Skira and the other festivals we celebrate; but if she gives birth to a coward or a crook, like a crooked trierarch or a rotten helmsman, she ought to sit at the back, with her hair clipped round a pudding-basin, behind the mother of the hero. What right

840 has the city got to let Hyperbolus' mother – and her a money-lender – sit all clothed in white, with her hair down, next to Lamachus' mother?

CA 121 ARISTOPHANES, *Lysistrata* 638–651

638 CHORUS OF WOMEN. Listen all you citizens, as we utter words useful to the state; and rightly, since it nurtured us in splendour and glory. When I was seven, I carried the sacred symbols; then at ten I was grinder of

645 Athena's barley; then at the Brauronian festival of Artemis, I was the Bear-girl in the saffron robe; and when I had grown up handsome, I

648 carried the sacred basket, wearing a necklace of dried figs. Surely I have a right to give good advice to the city. But don't hold it against me that I'm a woman if I produce something to cope with the present situation. I do my bit; I pay my contribution in men.

On the Brauronia, see H. W. Parke: *Festivals of the Athenians* pp. 139–141.

CA 122 XENOPHON, *Memorabilia* 2.2.9–10

(*Socrates takes Lamprocles to task for criticising his mother*)

9 "You know perfectly well that whatever your mother may say to you, she intends you no harm; in fact she wants you to do better than anyone else. And yet you complain about her. Do you really think she is ill-disposed towards you?"

"Certainly not."

10 "So she is well-disposed towards you, she looks after you as well as she can when you are ill, to see that you are restored to health and want for nothing, she offers numerous prayers and vows on your behalf to win blessings from the gods; and yet you say she is a nuisance! In my opinion, if you find a mother like that unendurable, you'd find any blessing unendurable."

CA 123 EURIPIDES, *Medea* 1081–1089

CHORUS OF CORINTHIAN WOMEN. Often now I have engaged in intelligent discussions, and entered into arguments more than a woman would want to; but we too have some cultural awareness (*mousa*) which contributes to our intellect. Not all of us. But here and there you may be able to find one or two women who are not completely ignorant (*apomousos*).

This and the following excerpt support the view that women could attend the dramatic festivals.

124 PLATO, *Laws* 658a–d (much abbreviated)

(Suppose there were a competiton open to performers of every kind in which the prize was awarded simply to the entry giving the most pleasure, how should we decide who had won?)

d   If the verdict rested with little children, they will certainly go for the conjuror; older children will go for comedies; tragedy will be the favourite of educated women and young men and perhaps the general majority.

CA 125 ATHENAEUS 12.534c

Alcibiades was handsome in appearance and looked after his hair till well into adult life, and wore peculiar shoes called after him Alcibiadeans. When he was presenting a chorus he would enter the theatre in the procession wearing a purple cloak, and was admired not only by men but also by women.

Husbands and wives:

CA 126 EURIPIDES, *Trojan Women* 643–656

ANDROMACHE. I aimed at being held in high esteem, but have now lost all the good that I won. I worked hard in the house of Hector to achieve all

648   that is thought good in women. First of all I stayed indoors, and put aside any desire for going out – which gets one a bad name whether or not one deserves it. And I would not let smart female gossip inside the house; but I was content with the wise counsel of my own mind which my upbringing had given me. In the presence of my husband, my

655   tongue was still, my look was demure. I knew when to overrule my husband, and when to yield to him.

CA 127 XENOPHON, *Economicus* 7.4–6, 23–25, 35–37, 42

4   "Tell me, Ischomachus, did you train your wife yourself to be as you wanted her, or did she come from her parents already able to manage her proper duties?"

5   "She was not yet 15 when she came to me, and all her life until then she had been very carefully looked after, so that she might hear, see and say as

6   little as possible. What then could she have known? Wouldn't you think it enough if when she came she just knew how to produce a cloak from the wool given her, and seen the spinning given to the maids?"

(*Ischomachus goes on to explain how providentially men and women are made to help each other*)

23   "God made the heart and body of men better able to endure cold and heat and long journeys and campaigns. So he enjoined outdoor activities upon man. But upon woman he apparently enjoined indoor ones because

24   he made her less physically able to stand up to such things. Then, aware of

having given woman the task of looking after new-born children, he gave
25 her a larger share than the man of love for new-born infants. Then because
he had given her the additional task of guarding the stores, God
consciously made woman more apprehensive than man, knowing that it is
no bad thing for a guardian to have an apprehensive disposition."

(*Finally Ischomachus lists his wife's duties*)

35 "You will have to stay inside and help in sending out the servants with
36 outdoor tasks; you must supervise the indoor servants, and receive any
revenues; from these you must meet any necessary expenses, and look
after the surplus providently, so that you don't spend the whole year's
budget in a month. When wool is brought to you, you must see that the
right clothes are made for those who need them. And you must see that the
37 dried corn remains fit for consumption. There is also one duty that may
not appeal to you much – looking after any servant who falls ill."

"Oh, no, that will be a great pleasure" she said.

(*The wife is also expected to undertake the training and disciplining of
some of the servants*)

42 "But what will give you the most pleasure will be to show yourself better
than me, and make me your servant; you need not fear that you will be less
esteemed in the household as the years pass, but you can be confident that
as you get older and become a better guardian of the household and
partner for me and the children, you will be held in ever higher esteem."

CA 128 XENOPHON, *Economicus* 10.2

"Once" said Ischomachus "I saw my wife had anointed herself heavily
with white lead to make herself look paler than she was, and with alkanet
to heighten the natural red in her cheeks; she was also wearing high
platform soles to make herself look taller."

(*Ischomachus persuades his wife that she looks more attractive without
cosmetics, and suggests that if she wants to enhance her beauty, she should
do her housework more vigorously*)

CA 129 LYSIAS 1.6–10

6 When I decided to marry, gentlemen, and brought a wife into the house, I
was generally disposed not to harass her or be too repressive about her
doing what she wanted, and I looked after her as well as I could and was
properly attentive: by the time my child was born, I already had trust in
her and I put all my resources at her disposal, thinking this the truest
expression of the close tie between us.
7 At first, gentlemen, she was superb – a clever housekeeper, thrifty and
exact in her stewardship. It was my mother's death that was the start of
8 my troubles. When she was carried out to burial, my wife went with the
cortege, was seen by the defendant and eventually seduced. He used to
wait for her maid as she came to market and got messages through to her
and brought about her downfall.
9 In the first place I must explain that I have a small house on two floors,
of equal size upstairs and downstairs, that is in the women's and the men's
quarters. When our child was born, its mother suckled it, and so that she

10   shouldn't risk coming down the stairs whenever she wanted to wash, I
      started to live upstairs and the women down below. This custom became
      established, so that my wife often went below to the child to sleep, so that
      she could give it the breast and stop it crying. This went on for a long time
      and I never suspected anything but was simple enough to suppose that my
      wife was the most chaste in town.

CA 130 PLUTARCH, *Alcibiades* 8.2–4

2   Some say that it was not Hipponicus, but Callias his son who gave
      Hipparete in marriage to Alcibiades with a dowry of ten talents. Then,
      when she produced a child, Alcibiades demanded a further ten talents,
      saying that this was part of the agreement. Callias was afraid of his
      machinations, and declared that his money and house was to go to the
3   state if he chanced to die without leaving an heir. Hipparete was well
      behaved and fond of her husband, but so distressed by his extra-marital
      affairs with foreign and Athenian women (*hetairai*) that she left home and
      went to live with her brother. Alcibiades continued to indulge himself
      without giving her a thought, until she was driven to lodge a petition for
      divorce with the magistrate – not through intermediaries, but in her own
4   person. When she appeared for the purpose, as the law required, Alci-
      biades came up and seized her; then dragged her off home with him
      through the agora, with no one daring to try and stop him or get her away.
      In fact she stayed with him until her death which happened not long
      afterwards.

CA 131 DIOGENES LAERTIUS 2.36–37

(*Socrates' matrimonial situation*)

To Xanthippe, when she was first abusing him, but later actually poured
water over him, he said "Didn't I say that when Xanthippe was thunder-
ing she'd cause rain too?" To Alcibiades' remark that Xanthippe was
insufferable when she was abusing him he said "But I am used to it, just as
37   if I was continually hearing a windlass working: and can you" he went on
      "bear the sound of cackling geese?" When he replied "But they produce
      eggs and young for me", he said "So does Xanthippe bear children for
      me."
         Once when she actually took away his cloak in the market-place, his
      acquaintances advised him to lay hands on her. "Oh yes" he said, "so that
      while we are sparring each of you may say 'Bravo, Socrates! Well done,
      Xanthippe!'?" He used to say that he lived with a harsh wife as horse-
      trainers do with spirited horses. "But as they," he said "after mastering
      these easily get the better of the rest, so I too through experience of
      Xanthippe will adapt myself to everyone else."

CA 132 ANDOCIDES 1.124–129

124   Now just consider the circumstances of the birth of this son, to whom
      Callias tried to assign Epilycus' daughter, and how he begot him. It is a
      good story, gentlemen. He married Ischomachus' daughter, but after
      living with her for less than a year, he took her mother too, and the villain

lived with the two of them, acting as priest to Mother and Daughter and
125 keeping both mother and daughter in his house. For his part he was
unashamed and cocked a snook at Demeter and Persephone: but Ischomachus' daughter, thinking death preferable to witnessing these goings-
on, tried to strangle herself but was prevented in mid-act, and when she
recovered she fled the house, and so the mother displaced the daughter.

Callias then fell out with the mother in turn and got rid of her too. She
said she was pregnant by him: but when she bore a son, he denied it was
126 his. So the woman's relatives took the child and came to the altar at the
Apaturia with a sacrificial victim and told Callias to begin the ceremony.
He asked whose the child was. "The son of Callias, son of Hipponicus"
they said. "That's me" he said. "Yes, and he's your child" they replied.
Whereupon he grasped the altar and swore that he had never had a son
apart from Hipponicus by Glaucon's daughter . . .
127 Well, after a while he fell in love again with the shameless old mother
and took her back into his house, and he took the child, now quite grown
up, to the *Kêrukes*, saying he was his. Calliades opposed his being given
the child, but the *Kêrukes* voted in accordance with their laws that a father
who swore that a child was his should take him. Callias held the altar and
swore that the child was his true-born son by Chrysias . . .
128 Is there any Greek precedent, gentlemen, for a man marrying a woman
and then marrying the mother and the mother supplanting the daughter?
And now, while living with the mother, he wants to take Epilycus'
daughter, so that the granddaughter can supplant the grandmother!
129 Finding a name for his son is surely going to defy the nimblest wits. The
father has lived with these three generations of women, and the boy, he
says, is son of the first which means brother of the second and uncle of the
third. What are we to call him? Oedipus? Aegisthus?

Wives and Mistresses:

CA 133 ISAEUS 3.13–14

13 That the woman whom this man says he betrothed to our uncle was the
mistress of anyone who wanted her and no wife of our uncle, has been
testified by the rest of the household and the neighbours: they confirm that
whenever this man's sister was with my uncle, she was accompanied by
14 fights and revels and much licentious behaviour. I hardly need to tell you
that no one would have the nerve to engage in revels with a married
woman, nor do married women accompany the men at banquets or dine
with strangers – and casual strangers at that. . . .

CA 134 PLUTARCH, *Pericles* 24.1–5

1 But since Pericles is thought to have made the expedition against the
Samians in order to gratify Aspasia, this seems to be a good point at which
to deal with the question of that woman – what skill or power she
possessed which enabled her to get the better of the foremost politicians
and to give no trivial or insignificant account of herself to the
philosophers.

2   It is agreed that she was a Milesian by race, the daughter of Axio-
3   chus ... Some say that she was taken up by Pericles because she was clever
       and political. Indeed there were times when Socrates came to visit her with
       his acquaintances, and his intimates would bring their wives to hear her,
       although she presided over a business that was neither decent nor
4   respectable – bringing up young girls to be prostitutes. Aeschines
       however claims that Lysicles the sheep-dealer, of low birth and base
       nature, came to be the first of the Athenians from having lived with
       Aspasia after the death of Pericles. In Plato's *Menexenus* however, even if
       the first chapters have been written in light-hearted vein, there is this much
       authenticated information in it, that the woman had the reputation of
       consorting with many of the Athenians on the subject of rhetoric.
5   However it is clear that Pericles' affection for Aspasia was physical. For
       he had a wife who was related to him by ties of kinship. She however had
       previously lived with Hipponicus, by whom she had Callias the Wealthy.
       As Pericles' wife she also gave birth to Xanthippus and Paralus. After-
       wards however, as their life together was not agreeable, he handed her
       over, with her consent, to another, and he himself took Aspasia and
       treated her with unusual affection.

Prostitution:

CA 135 AESCHINES 1.119

Demosthenes ... expresses great surprise that the *Boulê* every year farms
out the prostitution tax, and that those who buy the right to collect it
know exact details of the men who ply this trade.

CA 136 DEMOSTHENES 59.32–33

32   *Evidence: Philagrus testifies that he was present in Corinth when Phryn-*
       ion ... laid down 20 minas to pay for the defendant Neaera to Timanorides
       of Corinth and Eucrates of Leucas. And when he had paid he went off with
       Neaera to Athens.
33   On arriving with her at Athens Phrynion used her in vulgar and
       unrestrained fashion, taking her with him to dinners wherever he went and
       drank, and she was always living it up with him and openly copulating
       with him everywhere whenever he wanted; for he thought this licentious-
       ness increased his prestige in the eyes of the beholders. Among others to
       whom he took her ... was Chabrias ... on the occasion when he had won
       the four-horse chariot-race at Delphi (*in 373*) ... and on his return was
       holding a victory-feast at Colias. There many people lay with her when she
       was drunk and Phrynion was asleep, among them the waiters at Chabrias'
       table.

Economic pressures on women:

CA 137 ARISTOTLE, *Politics* 1300a

Superintendents of children or women and officers with similar responsibilities are a mark of aristocracy: they are not democratic, for how in a

democracy can one prevent the women of the poor (from leaving their houses?) nor oligarchic (the women of oligarchs wouldn't stand for it).

CA 138 ARISTOPHANES, *Thesmophoriazusae 443–458*

(The speaker is one of the women meeting to complain about Euripides' misrepresentation of them in his plays)

I have only a few words to say ... My husband died in Cyprus, leaving me with five little children, whom I brought up with difficulty, weaving chaplets in the myrtle-market. For a while we got by – pretty poorly it's
450 true; but now this man by his tragedies has persuaded men that there are no gods; so we can no longer sell even half as much. So now I support you all, and agree that there are many reasons for punishing the man; his
455 treatment of us has been bad, as bad as the vegetables among which he was brought up. But I must be off to the agora. I've got an order of twenty chaplets to see to for my customers.

(Euripides' mother was popularly represented as a greengrocer).

CA 139 XENOPHON, *Memorabilia 2.7.8, 10–12*

(Aristarchus is complaining that he cannot support his womenfolk; Socrates encourages him to put them to work producing goods for sale. For the context, see CA 39)

8 "Did these women learn what you say they understand as if it was something of no practical value, and they were going to make no use of it; or did they intend to take it seriously and try to get some benefit out of
10 it? ... It looks as if their knowledge is of a genteel kind, most suitable for women. And everyone works with the greatest ease, speed, pride and satisfaction at what they understand. So get them going; you will all profit by it, and they will probably be quite happy to acquiesce."

11 "That is a most excellent suggestion" said Aristarchus. "Until now I haven't wanted to get a loan because I knew that I would be unable to repay the money once I had spent it; but now I think I shall risk it, to get the business started."

12 The capital that he thereby obtained enabled him to purchase wool. The women worked through the morning meal and only had supper when their work was done; they became cheerful instead of sulky, and regarded each other with happiness instead of suspicion; they loved Aristarchus as their guardian, and he was happy with them because they were helping.

CA 140 DEMOSTHENES 57.30–31, 34

(The speaker is Euxitheus, protesting against his removal from the roll of citizens)

30 My father then was clearly born at a time when, even if he was of Athenian descent on only one side, he could claim to be a citizen; for he was born before Euclides' archonship *(403)*. As to my mother ... Eubulides' accusations contravene not only decrees of the assembly about the Agora, but also the laws which state that a man is liable to a charge of slander if he maligns the trade conducted in the Agora by any citizen, male
31 or female. We admit that, regrettable life though it is, we are sellers of

headbands. But if, Eubulides, you take this as evidence that we are not Athenians, let me remind you that, on the contrary, no foreigner is allowed to run a business in the Agora.

34   . . . If my mother was a foreigner, he should have produced as witnesses people who had examined the tax-registers in the Agora to see whether she paid the foreigners' tax and where she came from: or if she was a slave, he should have produced preferably the buyer or, failing him, the seller, or in the last resort someone else to testify either that she was a slave or had been freed.

CA 141 DEMOSTHENES 57.45

(My mother was a wet-nurse . . .) Even if being a wet-nurse is demeaning, I will not shirk the truth. . . . Poverty forces free citizens to take up many slavish and humiliating occupations, which should prompt pity rather than further disaster. I hear that, because of the fluctuating fortunes of the city in those days, many female citizens have become wet-nurses or weavers or grape-pickers, and many are now rich instead of poor.

III. CIVIC LIFE

(a) POLITICS – see LACTOR 5

(b) THE LAW

For detailed treatment, see esp. A. R. W. Harrison: *The Law of Athens*, vol. 2.

1. Institution of Legal Proceedings (CA 142–161)

The responsibility for bringing actions to court lay with the individual. In the case of public suits (*graphai*) affecting the state, any individual could initiate proceedings; in private suits (*dikai*) it was up to the injured party. For certain offences there was a summary procedure of arrest for those caught in the act; but in most cases a summons was delivered to the accused naming a day for appearance before the magistrate (this was the procedure under which Alcibiades was haled from Sicily in 415, Thuc. 6.61.4–5), and a deposit paid by the plaintiff. If the magistrate accepted the case, a preliminary hearing would take place at which oaths were exchanged and the defendant could enter a counter-plea. Finally the case would be assigned to an appropriate court and jurors allocated. If the plaintiff failed to get to court himself, or to win one fifth of the votes, he was penalised.

CA 142 DEMOSTHENES 21.32

You are aware that these *Thesmothetae* are not known as individuals by the name of *Thesmothetês* but each by his own name whatever it is. Well, if someone assaults one of them or abuses him as a private individual, such a man will have to defend a public suit for wanton attack or a private suit for abuse; but if the same man so treats a *Thesmothetês*, he will lose all his citizen rights once for all. The reason is that in so doing he is also assaulting the laws and the crown conferred by you as a body and the name of the city: for *Thesmothetês* is a name which belongs not to any individual but to the city.

(*For the functions of Thesmothetae, see CA 145*)

CA 143 DEMOSTHENES 21.47

(*Quotation of Law*)

If someone commits wanton attack against another, child, woman or man, free or slave, or acts illegally against any such person, any Athenian with the right to do so shall, if he wishes, indict the offender before the *Thesmothetae*, who shall arraign the offender before the *Hêliaea* within 30 days of the indictment unless a public emergency intervenes, and, if it does, at the first possible opportunity afterwards. The *Hêliaea* shall fix immediately the penalty for anyone it condemns and decree what he is to suffer or pay. Whoever brings a private indictment under the law shall, if he does not proceed with it or if, proceeding, he fails to win a fifth of the votes, pay 1000 drachmas to the public treasury. And if he is fined for his offence and it is against a free man, he shall be imprisoned until he pays.

(*The Hêliaea is the Athenian people sitting as a jury-court*)

CA 144 ARISTOTLE, *Constitution of Athens 56.6–7*

6 Applications to bring public or private suits must go to the Archon, who scrutinises them before allowing them to court, in the following cases: wrongful treatment of parents (such suits are without risk of penalty to the prosecutor) or of orphans (these suits are against the guardians) or of an heiress (these are against her guardians and those dwelling with her) or of an orphan's house (again against the guardians): insanity, if someone accuses another of ruining his estate while insane: the selection of liquidators, if someone does not want to give his property to the state: the establishment of wardships, and settlement of disputed claims to the same: the production of persons or things in open court: the entering of his own
7 name as guardian: claims to inheritances and heiresses. He exercises general supervision over orphans, heiresses, and women who claim to be pregnant by a dead husband; and he has the power to fine offenders or bring them to court. He rents out the houses of orphans and of heiresses until they reach the age of 14 and collects the rents: and he is the official who makes guardians provide children with food if they fail to do so.

(*For heiresses, see CA 73–76*)

CA 145 ARISTOTLE, *Constitution of Athens 59.1–6*

1 The *Thesmothetae* are first responsible for publishing the days on which the courts are to sit; secondly for giving these dates to the magistrates,
2 who act accordingly. They also bring impeachments before the Assembly and introduce condemnations by show of hands and present all cases there: also accusations of illegal or unsuitable legislative proposals, impeachments of presiding magistrates or chairmen, examinations of the
3 record of the generals. They also handle public suits involving court fees, cases of aliens improperly (through bribery, or otherwise) gaining citizen status, accusations of malicious informing, bribery, false entry, false

4

5

6

subscription to a summons, failure to cancel a debt, or wrongful cancellation of it, and adultery. They introduce the examinations of all magistrates before entering an office and handle those rejected by their fellow demesmen and condemnations coming from the Council. They also introduce private suits relating to the mart or the mines or slaves who swear at a free man. And they assign by lot to the magistrates courts for private and public cases. They are also in charge of contracts with other states and introduce cases arising therefrom, and of accusations of perjury coming from the Areopagus.

CA 146 HARPOCRATION, under *Impeachment (eisangelia)*

For crimes affecting the people, of the greatest kind and requiring immediate action, and over which there is no control and no laws laid down for the authorities under which they can prosecute, but the charge is first laid before the Council or the people, and for which the heaviest penalties are laid down for the defendant if he is convicted, and the plaintiff is not penalised even if he loses, unless he fails to get one fifth of the votes; then he has to pay 1000 dr.

CA 147 DEMOSTHENES 22.26–27

26

27

(*Solon provided several legal ways of obtaining redress against an offender.*) Take for instance theft. A strong and self-confident man can arrest the thief, at the risk of a fine of 1000 drachmas for wrongful arrest: a man of lesser physique can lead the archons to him and they will arrest him. If neither course pleases you, you can bring an indictment. Or a more diffident victim, too poor to risk a fine of 1000 drachmas, can bring a suit before an arbitrator and so avoid the risk.

CA 148 LYSIAS 13.85–86

85

86

I gather Agoratus is attaching weight to the fact that the words "caught in the act" were added to the warrant for his arrest. This is ridiculous, – as if, had the words not been added, his arrest would be in order, but since they have been added, he has some loophole. This is as much as to admit that he did kill, but was not caught in the act, and to claim that therefore he should be let off. I think that the Eleven who accepted his arrest, never supposing that they were helping Agoratus who was insistent on his plea even then, emphatically did the right thing in compelling Dionysius, when he laid the accusation, to add the words "in the act".

CA 149 ARISTOTLE, *Constitution of Athens* 52.1

They also appoint the Eleven by lot to supervise those in prison and to put to death arrested thieves, kidnappers of slaves, and robbers – that is if they confess; if they dispute the matter, the Eleven have to take them to court, to release them, if acquitted, and otherwise then put them to death.

CA 150 LYSIAS 6.11–12

11

But Andocides so despised the gods and the vengeance owed to them that before he had been ten days in Athens he brought a suit for impiety before the *Archôn Basileus* and obtained permission to proceed – this was his record in matters concerning the gods: and this will make you sit up – he claimed Archippus was guilty of impiety against his (Andocides') hereditary bust of Hermes. Archippus claimed in reply that the Hermes was certainly safe and sound and had not suffered the fate of the other Hermae; all the same to avoid trouble from Andocides, knowing the sort of man he was, he settled by paying compensation in cash.

12

CA 151 DEMOSTHENES 58.1

Since our father, thanks to Theocrines here, fell foul of the city to the extent of being condemned to pay ten talents, and this sum being doubled, we were completely ruined, I determined with your aid, gentlemen of the Jury, to get even with him and let neither my youth nor anything else stop my laying this information (*endeixis*) against him.

CA 152 ARISTOPHANES, *Wasps* 1415–1426

(*Philocleon has been indulging in a drunken spree, and the legal consequences are now catching up with him*)

1415 BDELYCLEON. Here comes another one to summons you, it seems: at any rate he's got a summons witness (*klêtêr*) with him.

PLAINTIFF. Oh dear, not my lucky day. Old man, I summons you for assault.

BDELYCLEON. Please, please don't summons him I beg you. I'll pay you compensation for him, whatever you determine, and with my compliments too.

1421 PHILOCLEON. No, *I'll* be glad to settle the matter with him. I admit to the battery. But just step over here. Will you leave it to me to decide how much I must pay for the action, to be reconciled for the future, or are you going to tell me?

1426 PLAINTIFF. You say; I don't want any law-suits or actions.

CA 153 ARISTOPHANES, *Clouds* 1131–1141

STREPSIADES. Five, four, three, two, then straight after that the day I fear
1135 and hate most of all – the last and first day. Then everyone to whom I happen to owe anything puts down his court-deposit (*prytaneion*) and says with an oath that he will destroy me utterly and completely; and
1138 when I ask with all sweet reason and justice: "Please, my good man, don't ask for it all at once; put some of it off; let me off a bit", they say they'll never get anything back that way; they abuse me for a villain and say they'll take me to court.

CA 154 ISAEUS 6.12

In the preliminary hearing (*anakrisis*) before the archon when they paid their deposit and laid their claim on behalf of these children as being the true-born children of Euctemon, we asked them who the children's mother was and whose daughter she was, but they could not point to anyone, despite our protests and the archon's order that they should answer in accordance with the law.

CA 155 XENOPHON *Symposium* 5.2

(*Socrates challenges Critobulus to a beauty contest*)

"As the first stage of my suit, I summon you to a preliminary examination (*anakrisis*). So answer my questions."

CA 156 POLLUX 8.55–56

(*From a passage explaining legal terminology*)

56 The preliminary oath (*proômosia*) is the one which the plaintiff swears, to the effect that his accusation is genuine; the counter-oath (*antômosia*) is the one sworn by the defendant to the effect that he has done no wrong.

CA 157 ISOCRATES 18.2–3

2 Since on your return from Piraeus (*in 403*) you saw some of your fellow-citizens eager to bring false accusations and violate the Amnesty (*see CA 445*), to stop them and to show others that you had made this covenant not under duress but in the public interest, you made a law on the proposal of Archinus that if anyone goes to law contrary to his oath, the defendant shall be allowed to enter a demurrer and the archons shall hear

3 this case first when the man entering the demurrer shall speak first, and whoever loses the case shall pay a fine of one sixth of the potential damages.
      (*On the problems of the demurrer (paragraphê) see Harrison pp. 106–124*)

CA 158 DEMOSTHENES 47.45

When Theophemus refused to refer to independent judgement the matter of the blows he had given me (on the mouth), I brought a summons against him and was given leave to bring a private case for assault. He brought a counter-summons, but when the case was before the arbitrators and their verdict was imminent, he started entering a demurrer and applying for postponement and I, confident that I was in the right, came before your court.

CA 159 Scholiast on ARISTOPHANES, *Wasps* 88

The number of jurors was 500; at one time they were given two obols, but later when Cleon was general, at the height of the Peloponnesian War, he instituted the three-obol fee.

(On jurors see also LACTOR 5 pp. 22–26. The total number on the panel each year was 6,000)

CA 160 LYSIAS 13.35

When the Thirty were established, they immediately set about trying these men in the *Boulê*, though the people had voted for trying them in a court before a jury of 2,000.

CA 161 DEMOSTHENES 58.6

This law states explicitly for those choosing to indict or denounce someone . . . the terms under which this must be done – namely that if the accuser goes to court and fails to win a fifth of the votes he shall pay 1000 dr. and if he fails to go to court at all, another 1000 dr.

2. Rules of Evidence (CA 162–172)

Cases were conducted under the presidency of a magistrate, who did not however act in the capacity of a judge. The bulk of the trial was in the form of speeches by the litigants (perhaps written for them by professionals like Lysias), and by their supporters who would speak for their character. These speeches were limited in time by the use of a water-clock so that the proceedings could be completed in a single day. Evidence was admitted in the form of citation of laws, written documents and depositions, and the spoken testimony of witnesses. Evidence from slaves was only admitted under torture. All possible care was taken to maintain the integrity of evidence (hearsay was not admitted), but there is no doubt that mass juries were equally susceptible to rhetorical and emotional appeal.

CA 162 ANDOCIDES 1.150

(The conclusion of Andocides' speech On the Mysteries)

And now it is time for those men who have already given clear proof of their outstanding virtue to the state, to come up here and tell you what they know about me. Hear then Anytus, Cephalus, and Thrasyllus and the rest of my fellow-tribesmen who have been picked out to speak for me.

CA 163 DEMOSTHENES 26.24

It would be ridiculous . . . if, having decreed the death-penalty for the citation of a non-existent law, you were then to let off scot-free men who treat existing laws as if they were non-existent.

CA 164 DEMOSTHENES 49.43

Of the fact that Timotheus was left owing us this money . . . you have heard the evidence of my brother and of Phormio who gave it and I was prepared to enter an assurance on oath. But Timotheus challenged me to go before an arbitrator and demanded that I should bring the records from the bank and asked for transcripts and sent Phrasierides to the bank.

So I produced the records for Phrasierides to examine and record what Timotheus owed.

CA 165 DEMOTHENES 46.9–10

9   The laws forbid a man to be his own witness ... in the following terms:
10   "Litigants shall answer questions asked by the opponent but shall not give evidence." ...

Furthermore the law states: "A charge of perjury shall hold against anyone who gives evidence illegally."

CA 166 ISAEUS 3.19–21

19   You all know that when we are going to foreseeable transactions which require witnesses, we take along with us those closest to us; but for sudden
20   and unforeseen events we all use as witnesses those on the spot. And for direct testimony we are bound to use as witnesses the bystanders in person, of whatever sort they are; but if we are taking depositions from the sick or from persons about to go abroad, we all take along with us for preference the most respectable of our fellow citizens and those best
21   known to us, and we take the deposition before as many witnesses as possible, so that he who deposes shall not later deny his evidence and that you shall have honest and reliable witnesses to his evidence whom you can trust.

(*See CA 62 for action that could be taken against a reluctant witness*)

CA 167 DEMOSTHENES 57.4

I supposed it was the duty of Eubulides and all others who bring accusations aimed at disfranchisement to state accurately what they know and not bring any hearsay evidence to this sort of trial. Such conduct has long been so emphatically adjudged wrong, that the laws do not allow hearsay evidence in support of even the most trivial charges.

Evidence under torture:

CA 168 ISAEUS 8.12

Both in private and in public you (jurors) regard torture as the best test of the truth; and wherever slaves and free men are jointly concerned in some matter under investigation, rather than use the testimony of the free men, you prefer to discover the truth by torturing the slaves.

CA 169 ANTIPHON 2.3.4

They are wrong in saying that the evidence of the attendant is unreliable. A slave is not tortured for evidence of this kind (*viz. as witness to an assault*); he is let free. It is when he denies a theft or joins his master in concealing something that we expect him to tell the truth under torture.

CA 170 ANDOCIDES 1.64

To prove this, I offered my slave under torture to say that I was ill and did not even leave my bed . . .

Pressures on the jury:

CA 171 DEMOSTHENES 19.1

The strong partisan feelings aroused by this case must have been obvious to all of you, gentlemen, when you saw just now the press of people jostling you as you drew your lots. I must entreat all of you to remember your duty to put no cause or individual before justice and the oath you have each sworn.

CA 172 PLUTARCH, *Pericles* 32.1,3

1 About this time Aspasia was standing trial for impiety. Hermippus the comic poet brought the charge against her, and also accused her of making assignations for Pericles with freeborn women. Diopithes introduced a proposal for the indictment of those who did not believe in the gods, or for expounding theories about the heavens; he was trying to
3 direct suspicion at Pericles through Anaxagoras. . . . In fact Pericles begged Aspasia off by shedding many tears on her behalf, so Aeschines claims, throughout the proceedings, and by pleading with the jurors.

(*For other emotional appeals see Aristophanes' Wasps 563–74*) (*LAC-TOR 5 p.24*)

3. Execution of Judgement (CA 173–183)

In a case where there was no statutory punishment laid down, or where the damages had not already been fixed (as they would be in contractual claims for instance), one third of the day was assigned to assessing the penalty a guilty man had to pay: this might be death, imprisonment, loss of rights (see e.g. Andocides 1.75, LACTOR 5 p.39), or the payment of money. In private suits it was up to the individual to secure execution of judgement in his favour: he could seize disputed property or distrain upon goods to the same value. Once a case had been decided, it could not be reopened, and there was no equivalent of the modern appeal procedure. However for political reasons the verdicts reached in public suits while the Thirty were in power were annulled the following year.

CA 173 XENOPHON, *Memorabilia* 1.2.62

The laws lay down the death penalty for people convicted of theft and larceny, picking pockets, housebreaking, kidnapping, and temple-robbing. And no one could have been further removed from all these categories than Socrates was.

CA 174 DEMOSTHENES 21.43

First, all laws dealing with injury lay down double recompense for voluntary injury, simple for involuntary. And this is reasonable. The sufferer is in any case entitled to compensation; but in punishing the perpetrator the law takes intent into account. Secondly the murder-laws punish deliberate killers with death or exile for life and with confiscation of property, whereas for involuntary killers they enjoin compassionate treatment.

CA 175 HARPOCRATION, under *Suits with and without assessment*

The suit with assessment is one in which there is no fixed amount of damages prescribed by law, but the jurors have to assess the penalty or compensation; the suit without assessment is the opposite – one in which no assessment is necessary because the amount has been determined by law.

CA 176 DEMOSTHENES 24.114

And even if a man steals a cloak or an oil-flask or some other trivial article from the Lyceum or the Academy or Cynosarges or pinches some bit of gear from the gymnasiums or the harbours, if it is above ten drachmas in value, Solon decrees the death-penalty. And if a man is convicted on a private charge of theft, Solon decrees a basic penalty of double compensation, with the rider that the court can impose a further penalty of five days and nights in chains, for all to see.

CA 177 DEMOSTHENES 27.67

If, God forbid, Aphobus is acquitted, I shall be liable to pay the standard fine, amounting to 100 minas. And Aphobus, if condemned, will have his penalty laid down by the court, and will pay it out of my money, not his; whereas my penalty is laid down by law.

(The standard fine, if the accuser failed to win one fifth of the votes, was one sixth of the damages claimed)

CA 178 DEMOSTHENES 43.71

(Quotation of Law)

If a man digs up an olive-tree at Athens, unless it is for a shrine of the Athenian state or one of the demes or for his own use up to two olive-trees a year or for use for the dead, he shall owe 100dr. per tree to the Treasury. A tithe of this shall belong to the Goddess. He shall also owe 100dr. per tree to the private citizen who prosecutes him.

CA 179 LYCURGUS, *Against Leocrates* 121

Hear this decree too, gentlemen, condemning anyone who absconded to Decelea during the war, and laying down that if any of them were caught returning, any Athenian could bring them before the *Thesmothetae*, who would take them in charge and hand them over to the executioner.

(For the Spartan occupation of Decelea in 413, see Thuc. 7.19,27)

CA 180 DEMOSTHENES 33.1

The law decrees that traders and ship-owners must seek redress before the *Thesmothetae* for any wrong done to them in the Mart or *en route* on the outward or the inward voyage; and lays down imprisonment as the penalty for offenders until they pay whatever they are condemned to pay. The object is to prevent random offences against traders.

CA 181 DEMOSTHENES 47.37

I once more asked him either in person to follow me to the naval magistrates and the Council and, if he denied the debt, to convince those who ordered the exaction of it, or else to return the ship's gear; otherwise, I said, I would take the gear as security, in accordance with laws and public decrees.

CA 182 DEMOSTHENES 24.54

(Quotation of Law)

Matters on which a verdict has already been given in court, whether ordinary suit or examination of conduct or judicial settlement, and whether the case is publicly or privately brought, or where state contracts are being farmed out, shall not be grounds for a further prosecution before a court; nor shall any of the archons allow a further vote on them, nor permit an illegal accusation.

CA 183 ANDOCIDES 1.88

You have decreed, Athenians, that the verdict in private suits and arbitrations (*diaitai*) shall be binding, if they were reached under the democracy, so that there should be no cancellation of debts or reversal of verdicts but that effect should be given to private contracts; while in all instances of public suit or denunciation (*phasis*) or information (*endeixis*) or arrest, you have decreed that only the laws passed since Euclides' archonship (*403*) shall be enforced.

(*For arbitrations, see Harrison pp. 64–68*)

IV. EDUCATION

(a) PRIMARY AND SECONDARY EDUCATION (CA 184–208)

The working of the Athenian democracy presumed an educated citizen body. Everyone was expected to be able to take part not only in the decision-making of the Assembly, but also in the administration of government on one of the many Boards of officials. However there does not seem to have been a legal requirement that children should go to school (unless one puts a very strict interpretation on Plato, *Crito* 50d, LACTOR 5 p.32). What the state did do was to legislate for the proper conduct of schools, provide incentives in the form of public competitions, and put up some of the necessary buildings (e.g. the public palaestras mentioned in Old Oligarch 2.10, LACTOR 2 p.7). But most of the responsibility for the provision and financing of education must have lain with the private individual.

Schooling started at the age of seven and might be continued as long as the parents could afford to maintain non-earning children. Once literacy had been achieved – and this was the main object of primary education – the pupil was given a thorough grounding in literature: this meant the works of the poets, epic, lyric and dramatic, with particular emphasis on Homer. The other subjects were physical education and music; technical education was provided through a system of craft-apprenticeship. Mathematics is notably absent from the curriculum, though a city of small traders cannot have been entirely innumerate, and complicated financial decrees were often being brought before the Assembly. Throughout the educational process there was much attention paid to moral instruction (this was one of the functions of the slave-tutor or *paidagôgos*), and the inculcation of liberal attitudes such as Pericles boasts of in the Funeral Speech.

CA 184 AESCHINES 1.9–11

The law-giver in dealing with the schoolmasters to whom we of necessity entrust our boys, despite the fact that their livelihood depends on their moral respectability, none the less clearly takes a precautionary attitude, laying down explicitly the hour at which a free boy must go to school, the

10 number of boys with whom he can enter and the time he must leave, and forbidding the masters and trainers to open their schools and gymnasia respectively before sunrise or to fail to shut them before sunset, viewing with deep suspicion the possibilities of deserted places and the dark. He also lays down what young men shall be allowed to attend the schools and of what age, and what magistrate shall see to these matters and supervise *paidagôgoi* ... Finally the law-giver lays down who shall be allowed to

11 consort with the boys and attend their cyclic dances, instructing that any *chorêgus* who wants to spend his money on these dances must be over forty years old, i.e. already morally at his most responsible, before he meets your children in this way.

CA 185 PLATO, *Timaeus* 21a–b

(*Critias speaking*)

Critias (my grandfather) was about 90 at the time, so he said, and I was

b about 10: it was the day during the Apaturia festival called Cureotis, and there was the usual competition for boys, when our fathers put up prizes for recitation. Many poems by many poets were recited, and Solon's ordinances being still new at the time, many of us boys competed in the singing of them.

CA 186 ARISTOTLE, *Politics* 1336a–b

So much for very early training of children: the next stage up to 5 years old, which is not yet suited to any formal learning or compulsory effort, if their growth is not to be impeded, nevertheless needs sufficient exercise to avoid physical sloth: this should be provided by various means, particularly play.... The superintendents of children should be particularly careful that children shall spend as little time as possible in the company of

b slaves. For children of this age and up to 7 years old must inevitably be brought up at home, and even at this age they are likely to pick up behaviour unsuited to a free man from what they hear and see.

CA 187 ARISTOTLE, *Politics* 1337b

There are four subjects in the usual syllabus for children, – letters, gymnastic, music and (for some) drawing. Letters and drawing are included because they are very useful for life; gymnastic because it trains the sinews for courage; but about the purposes of music there is room for doubt, for nowadays most people engage in it for the pleasure it gives, whereas it was originally put in the syllabus . . . because nature itself has a bent not only towards properly performed work but also towards well spent leisure.

(*On the place of music, see also CA 339–348*)

CA 188 XENOPHON, *Constitution of Sparta* 2.1

In Greek states other than Sparta, people who profess to give their sons the best education set servants over them as tutors (*paidagôgoi*) the moment they can understand what is said to them, and send them to teachers, to learn letters and music and the activities of the wrestling school.

CA 189 PLATO, *Lysis* 208c–d

c   SOCRATES. Do your parents let you look after yourself or won't they let you even do this?

LYSIS. They won't.

SOCRATES. So someone looks after you?

LYSIS. Yes, my *paidagôgos*.

SOCRATES. A slave?

LYSIS. Yes, of course: one of ours.

SOCRATES. It's shocking that a free man should be controlled by a slave. How does he do it?

LYSIS. By taking me to the teacher's, of course.

SOCRATES. And do these teachers also have charge of you?

LYSIS. Absolutely.

d   SOCRATES. So your father puts a whole host of masters and rulers over you?

(*The paidagôgos does however play an honourable part in Greek drama (e.g. in Sophocles' Electra)*)

CA 190 PLATO, *Alcibiades* 1.122b

– Whereas in your case, Alcibiades, Pericles put in charge of you as *paidagôgos* his most useless and senile house-slave, Zopyrus the Thracian. I could have gone further into the upbringing and education of the generals ranged against you . . .: but as for your own birth, upbringing and education, Alcibiades, (or those of any other Athenian), scarcely anyone bothers, unless you happen to have a lover.

CA 191 PLATO, *Politicus* 277e–278b

XENOS. We know that children, when they are first becoming acquainted with letters, discriminate the separate sounds in the shortest and easiest syllables and thus acquire the ability to give correct answers about the
278   sounds. . . . But when they meet these same sounds in other syllables they are once more confused and go wrong in thought and utterance. . . . The easiest and best way to lead them on to what they do not yet recognise is this – to take them back first to the work in which they formed a correct view of these same sounds and, having done so, to put
b   the old work alongside that which is not yet grasped and by comparison point out the essential likeness in the two sets of combinations, until as all the correctly understood sounds are displayed alongside those not understood they act as examples and make the children greet every sound (or letter) as having its own distinct and permanent identity in all syllables.

Some illiteracy still persisted however (See also CA 37).

CA 192 CRATINUS, fr. 122

No, mate, I can't read, not a letter. But I'll tell you from memory: I'm pretty good at remembering.

CA 193 PLATO, *Protagoras* 325c–326d

From his earliest childhood and for the rest of his life, there are people teaching a man and admonishing him. As soon as he understands what is said to him, his nurse, his mother, his *paidagôgos* and his father himself
d   strive to one end – to make the child as good as possible by instructing him in every deed and utterance and showing him that this is right and that is wrong, this honourable and that dishonourable, this acceptable to society and that not, that this he must do and that not do. And if he obeys, well and good: but if not, like a piece of wood which is being twisted and bent into shape they straighten him with threats and blows.

And then when they come to put him in the care of teachers they are much more concerned to instruct the teachers to ensure decent behaviour
e   in the boy than literacy or expertise in the lyre. That is what the teachers try to ensure: and when a boy does learn his letters and is ready to understand writings, as previously the spoken word, they set him to read
326   at his bench the poems of good poets and make him learn them by heart, – poems full of maxims and the description and praise and glorification of good men of the past, that the boy may emulate and imitate them and yearn to be like them himself.

The teachers of the lyre likewise aim at instilling a sense of decency and seeing that the young man does nothing bad: furthermore when he learns to play the lyre, they once again teach him the poems of further good
b   poets, writers to music, making him strictly observe the tunes and making the rhythms and harmonies second nature to the boy, so that he becomes

more civilised and, by acquiring a sure instinct for rhythm and harmony, more fit for utterance and action. For the whole life of man needs this instinct. Then again they send the boy to a physical trainer, so that he can

c   acquire a better physique with which to serve his noble mind and not be forced to quit through any feebleness of body in war or other similar ordeals.

    This is the action taken by those most able to do so, that is the rich: it is their sons who go to school earliest and leave latest. And when the boy leaves school, the city in turn makes him learn its laws and live by their

d   example and not simply live a selfish and unprincipled life; but just as teachers of writing draw with a stilus for children not yet expert in writing the outlines of letters before giving them the writing-tablet and make them follow the outlines when they write, so the city sets down the laws as guide-lines, laws apprehended by good law-givers of old, and makes men rule and be ruled in accordance with these laws and punishes anyone who transgresses them: and the name given to such punishment both in Athens and in many other cities is straightening, since this is the function of justice.

The circulation of books:

CA 194 EUPOLIS, fr. 304

I went around from garlic-sellers to onion-boys, from spice merchants to haberdashery, and to where books are for sale.

CA 195 XENOPHON, *Memorabilia* 4.2.1

Socrates discovered that the handsome Euthydemus had collected a great many works of the most famous among poets and sophists, and because of these supposed that he already excelled the boys of his age in wisdom, and moreover had high hopes of excelling everyone in rhetorical and political ability. Socrates noticed that Euthydemus was not yet going to the agora, because he was not old enough, but if he wanted to get anything done, he used to sit at one of the saddlers' shops near the agora; so Socrates too used to go to this shop with some of his companions.

CA 196 ALEXIS, fr. 135 (in Athenaeus 4.164b–c)

LINUS (*Heracles' tutor*). Go and help yourself, my boy, to any book you fancy reading. Take your time and have a good look at all the titles first. You'll find Orpheus there, and Hesiod, the Tragedians, Epicharmus, Homer, Choerilus, and every kind of work.
(*Heracles chooses a cookery-book*)

CA 197 ISOCRATES 4.159

I think that Homer's poetry owes its reputation partly to his noble praise of those who fought the barbarian, and that the motive of our ancestors in seeking to have his art honoured in poetry competitions and the education of the young was that by frequently hearing his lays we should recognise our natural enmity against the barbarian and in our admiration of the valour of the fighters emulate their exploits.

CA 198 XENOPHON, *Symposium* 3.5–6

5   "Now, Niceratus, you tell us on what kind of knowledge you pride yourself."

"My father" said Niceratus, "who saw to it that I should be a good man, made me learn all the poetry of Homer; even now I could say the whole of the *Iliad* and *Odyssey* by heart."

6   "But have you not noticed," said Antisthenes, "that all the rhapsodes know these poems too?"

"How could I fail to notice," said Niceratus, "seeing that I listen to them nearly every day?"

"Do you know any body of men," said Socrates, "more foolish than the rhapsodes?"

"No, by God," said Niceratus, "I don't think I do".

CA 199 PLUTARCH, *Alcibiades* 7.1

When he was passing beyond his childhood years, he presented himself before a school teacher and requested a book by Homer. When the teacher said he had nothing by Homer, he punched him with his fist and went on his way. When another asserted that he had a Homer, amended by himself, Alcibiades said: "Do you teach letters then, when you are capable of editing Homer?"

CA 200 PLATO, *Republic* 598d–e

Well then, we must consider tragedy and its leading exponent, Homer,
e   since we are told by some that such poets understand all arts and all human action from a moral point of view – come to that, all divine action too. For inevitably the good poet, if he is to produce successful creations, must understand what he is about.

CA 201 XENOPHON, *Symposium* 4.6

Thereupon Niceratus said: "Listen to me and you can learn how to improve yourselves. I am sure you know that Homer in his genius wrote about nearly everything that concerns man. So if any of you wants to know about housekeeping or public speaking or generalship, or be like Achilles or Ajax or Nestor or Odysseus, he had better cultivate me – because I know about all that kind of thing."

Physical Education (see also Aristophanes, *Clouds* 961ff., LACTOR 5 p.28):

CA 202 PLATO, *Lysis* 206d–e

Taking Ctesippus with me I went to the palaestra, the others following.
e   When we entered we found the boys had made the sacrifice and the sacred proceedings were almost complete, and everyone was playing at knuckle-bones and dressed in ceremonial garb. Most were playing outside the court but some were playing "odd and even" in a corner of the stripping-room with lots of knuckle-bones, picking them out of baskets, while others stood round them watching.

(For "odd and even" see CA 472)

CA 203 PLATO, *Politicus* 294d–e

XENOS. No doubt in your city, as in others, you have team-training for
running or something similar – training for victory.... So let us recall
the team-trainers' instructions in this sort of regime.... They think
there is no room for subtleties and attention to individual physical
e needs: instead they take a more broad and wholesale approach to their
physical-training system ... and require the same physical effort of the
whole team, starting them off, on their running or wrestling or
whatever it is, and stopping them all at the same time.

CA 204 ARISTOPHANES, *Knights* 985–996

CHORUS (*singing about Cleon*). I am also surprised at his hoggish taste in
music. His schoolmates say that he would often tune his lyre to the
Dorian mode, and refuse to learn any other. And then the music-
teacher would get angry and order him to get out, saying that the boy
was incapable of learning any harmony except the "Grease-my-
palmian".

For musical education, see also Aristophanes, *Clouds* 961 ff. (LACTOR 5 p.28),
and CA 339–348.

Technical education:

CA 205 XENOPHON, *Equestrianism* 2.2

Anyone who shares my views about training young horses will of course
farm the colt out. But he should only do so after making a note of what he
expects the horse to know when he is given back – as a man does when he
hands over his son for a craft-apprenticeship.

CA 206 PLUTARCH, *Solon* 22.1

(*Solon attempted to relieve the problems of over-population and lack of
exports at one stroke*)

He therefore directed the citizens towards the crafts, and introduced a law
to the effect that no son was obliged to support his father unless he had
been taught a craft.

CA 207 XENOPHON, *Memorabilia* 4.4.5

Socrates was saying how remarkable it was that if you wanted to
have someone taught the craft of the cobbler, the carpenter, the black-
smith or the equestrian, there was no shortage of people to send him
to for the purpose; but, to his knowledge, there was no one you could go
to if you wanted a course in Justice for yourself, your son, or your
servant.

The study of arithmetic seems to have been regarded rather as a special subject
(see Plato, *Protagoras* 318e, LACTOR 5 p.30).

CA 208 XENOPHON, *Memorabilia* 4.4.6–7

6 Socrates said: "You are so knowledgeable, Hippias, that I dare say you
never say the same thing twice even if the subject is the same."

"It's quite true that I always try to say something original."

7   "Even in things that you really know about? For instance if you were
asked how many letters there were in the name Socrates, and what they
were; or whether twice five is ten, would you give different answers at
different times?"

(b) THE SOPHISTS (CA 209–218)

Further education was offered in the teaching of the sophists. The term
"sophist" originally just meant an expert in any particular field, and even in the
Periclean period, when the meaning had narrowed to indicate a certain kind of
professional teacher, there was no uniformity about the subjects which they
used for the basis of their teaching. What most of them had in common was the
adoption of a rationalist approach to their subject, the positing of some moral
or political end, and the charging of uncommonly high fees. Two of the most
important influences on the emergent sophistic movement were the scientific
enquiries of the Presocratic philosophers of Ionia, and the development of new
rhetorical and argumentative techniques in Sicily.

Sophistic attitudes soon spread to almost all forms of intellectual activity, and
may be identified in many sections of the next four chapters. Popular opinion of
the sophists tended to be suspicious of their cleverness and troubled by their
scepticism; and the sophists' own views are in any case unfairly represented
since few of their writings survive, and our main testimony comes from Plato
who was extremely scornful of their pretensions.

CA 209 PLATO, *Protagoras* 316d–e

PROTAGORAS. I think the sophistic art is really an old one, but that the
ancient practitioners, being scared of its unpopularity, used cover
names, calling it poetry in the case of Homer for instance and Hesiod
and Simonides, or rites and prophecies in the case of the circle of
Orpheus or Musaeus: I have observed that some have even called it
gymnastic – Iccus of Tarentum, for instance, and the front-rank
e   sophist, still alive, Herodicus of Salymbria, originally of Megara; and
your Athenian Agathocles, a great sophist, used the cover-name of
music, and so did Pythoclides of Cos and many others. All of them, as I
say, used these other arts as disguises in their fear of unpopularity.

For Protagoras' educational objectives see Plato, *Protagoras* 318e–319a.
(LACTOR 5 p.30).

CA 210 PLUTARCH, *Themistocles* 2.4

There is more reason for supporting the view that Themistocles was a
disciple of Mnesiphilus the Phrearian, who was neither a rhetorician nor
one of the so-called natural philosophers, but had made a study of what
was called *sophia* (*lit.* = *wisdom*), a blend of political cleverness and
practical good sense, and so, you might say, preserved the principles
handed down from Solon. His successors married it to forensic skills, and

then, when they transferred their attention from action to words, they came to be called "sophists".

CA 211 PLUTARCH, *Pericles* 4.1–2

1   It is generally agreed that Pericles' teacher in the musical arts was Damon.... Damon was an out-and-out sophist, it seems, who had recourse to music as a screen to conceal his cleverness from the crowd; but
2   he associated with Pericles like a political trainer and masseur. Even so, though he used his lyre to veil his activities, Damon did not escape notice, but he was ostracised as an ambitious schemer and a lover of tyranny; and he provided a target for the shafts of the comic poets.

CA 212 PLATO, *Protagoras* 327e–328c

PROTAGORAS. .... If you enquired for an instructor in speaking Greek, you
328   wouldn't find one, nor would you readily find one for the instructing of craftsmen's sons in the crafts they have learned from their fathers, so far as their fathers and their fathers' friends in the craft could pass on their skill, whereas you would easily find one for inexperienced men. So it is with the teaching of virtue or anything else. All the same, if there is anyone who can even to a small degree help a man on the path to
b   virtue, that is something worthwhile. And I claim to be one such, and to help people more than the others towards becoming good, justifying the fee I charge and even more, as even my pupils would agree. For this reason in fact my method of charging a fee is as follows. Any pupil who is willing, pays my statutory fee: otherwise he can go to a shrine and
c   swear on oath how much he thinks the course is worth and put down a sum accordingly.

CA 213 PLATO, *Euthydemus* 271a–272b

271   CRITO. Who was it, Socrates, you were talking to yesterday in the Lyceum? There was a big crowd round you, so that although I wanted to listen, when I came up I could hear nothing distinctly. But I bent down and got a glimpse and I thought you were talking to a foreigner. Who was he?

SOCRATES. Which do you mean, Crito? There were two of them.

CRITO. The one I mean was next but one to you on your right. Between
b   you was Axiochus' young lad. He seemed to me to have come on a lot, Socrates. He must be much the same age as our Critobulus. But he is a slim chap. The man I mean looks well grown and handsome.

SOCRATES. That's Euthydemus. And the man on my left was his brother Dionysodorus. He too takes part in our converse.

CRITO. I don't know either of them, Socrates. They must be more new
c   sophists. Where do they come from? And what is their expertise?

SOCRATES. By birth they come, I think, from the Chios direction, but they migrated to Thurii, and then fleeing from there they have spent several years in this part of Greece. As to their expertise, it is marvellous, Crito. The two of them are complete all-rounders – I didn't realise before

d   what was meant by pancratiasts. They are absolutely armed at all
           points. They are not just like the two Acarnanian pancratiast brothers
           who could fight only with the body: these two are, first, very skilful
272   physically – they are clever at fighting in armour themselves and, for a
           fee, can teach others the art: secondly they are very good at fighting
           battles in the courts and at teaching others to speak and compose
           speeches suited to the courts. Previously these were their only ac-
           complishments, but now they have put the crown on the pancratiastic
           skill, and mastered the only remaining battlefield they had left unat-
           tempted, so that not a single man can lift a finger to them, so skilled
           have they become at fighting with words and refuting whatever is said,
b   untrue or true. I've a good mind, Crito, to hand myself over to them:
           for they claim within a short time to be able to pass on their skills to
           another.

CA 214 PLATO, *Hippias Major* 282b–e

           SOCRATES. Look at Gorgias, the sophist of Leontini – he came to Athens
           on a public embassy from Leontini as being the most efficient of his
           countrymen in handling politics. People thought he spoke very well in
           the assembly, and in private by giving oratorical displays and teaching
           the young he made a lot of money and took it home with him from
c   Athens. Or take if you like our friend Prodicus: he often came here on
           public missions, but when he last came here recently on a public
           mission from Ceos, he won high repute for a speech in the Council, and
           by his private displays and his instruction to the young received a
           staggering sum of money. But none of the sages of old ever expected to
           be paid money or to give displays of his own cleverness before a
d   conglomerate audience. They were too simple-minded and didn't
           realise how valuable money was. Whereas both the two I have
           mentioned earned more by their cleverness than any other craftsman
           from his craft: and before them there was Protagoras too.
           HIPPIAS. You don't know the half of it, Socrates. If you knew how much
           money I have made, you would be amazed. To take but one example,
e   when I came to Sicily and Protagoras was living there in high renown, a
           much older man than I, I earned in a short time much more than 150
           minas, and from one tiny place, Inycus, more than 20 minas. I took the
           money with me when I went home and gave it to my father: he and my
           other fellow-citizens were stunned. In fact I think I can say that I have
           earned more money than any two other sophists put together.

           (*For Gorgias see also CA 398 ff.*)

CA 215 PLUTARCH, *Moralia* 836e–f (*Lives of Ten Orators*)

e   Isocrates was the son of Theodorus of Erchia, a middle-class citizen who
           possessed slaves who made flutes. He grew rich on the proceeds, enough to
f   finance a chorus and educate his sons.... He was born in the 86th
           Olympiad, when Lysimachus was archon (*436*) ... As a child he received
           an education equal to that of any other Athenian, listening to Prodicus of
           Ceos, Gorgias of Leontini, Tisias of Syracuse, and the orator Theramenes.

(Tisias was, with Corax, one of the founders of the new Sicilian oratorical technique which Gorgias further developed)

CA 216 XENOPHON, *Memorabilia* 1.6.13

(Socrates to Antiphon the Sophist)

Those who sell wisdom for money to anyone who wants are called "sophists" – prostitutes you might say; but we regard it as proper conduct for a gentleman to befriend a person of quality by teaching him all the good he can.

CA 217 PLATO, *Republic* 493a

I am sure you would agree that all those money-making individuals whom people call "sophists" and reckon to be real professionals teach nothing more than the ideas which the majority hold when they are assembled together, and that is what they call wisdom.

CA 218 ARISTOPHANES, *Clouds* 92–118

STREPSIADES. You see this little house with the door in it?

PHIDIPPIDES. I do; what on earth is it, father?

95 STREPSIADES. It is the intellectuals' *phrontistêrium* (= *'think-tank'*). The people who live there maintain that heaven is shaped like a bread-oven, placed all round us as if we were coal. And they teach you how to win an argument whether it's right or wrong, if you pay them money.

100 PHIDIPPIDES. Who are they?

STREPSIADES. I don't know exactly what to call them; they're serious thinkers, good men and true.

PHIDIPPIDES. Ugh, a rotten lot, I know. You mean the pseuds with bare feet and pale faces, like Socrates and Chaerephon.

110 STREPSIADES. ... My dearest boy, I do wish you would go and take some lessons there.

PHIDIPPIDES. Tell me, what would I learn?

STREPSIADES. They are supposed to have two arguments, on any given subject, the better and the worse, and they claim to make the worse

116 prevail, even when it is in the wrong. So if you would go and learn this Unjust Argument for me, I wouldn't have to pay back to anyone a penny of the debts I've incurred on your behalf.

For a further example of popular hostility to sophism, see Plato, *Meno* 90e–92a, LACTOR 5 p.31.

V. RELIGION

(a) Ritual and Cult (CA 219–249)

Religion impinged upon the life of every Athenian. In its most public form it regaled him with the great state festivals which in the course of time had found a permanent place on the calendar (see Thuc.2.38.1); these gave him the only official holidays in the year (there were over forty of them, some lasting a full week), as well as providing the occasion for major athletic and dramatic competitions. The amount of public participation varied from the mere witnessing of symbolic rituals to the total involvement of the Mysteries, where initiation held promise of spiritual regeneration. On a smaller scale were the celebrations of the deme, the phratry and the family. Every household had its own altars for routine prayer and sacrifice, as well as the more elaborate rituals which marked the cycle of human life and death. The object of these acts of worship was usually one of the Olympian deities in a specific role, or, for more sinister purposes, one of the spirits of the underworld, including dead heroes, whose power in life was thought to extend beyond the grave. For those who felt that these rituals were now devoid of significance in a world where traditional values were crumbling, there was the attraction of the new ecstatic cults imported into the country in the last quarter of the century and most notably celebrated in Euripides' *Bacchae*.

CA 219 ARISTOPHANES, *Clouds* 615–619

> CHORUS (*Parabasis*). The moon says she treats you well, while you fail to keep your calendar straight, but jumble it all up, with the result that the gods get cross with her whenever they are cheated of their dinner and have to return home without enjoying the feast appointed for the day.

CA 220 ARISTOTLE, *Constitution of Athens* 57.1

> The *Archôn Basileus* first looks after the Mysteries together with superintendents appointed on show of hands by the people, two from the whole population of Athens, one from the Eumolpidae, one from the *Kêrukes*. Then he looks after the Lenaea, consisting of a procession and a competition. The procession is a joint responsibility of the *Archôn Basileus* and the superintendents, but he alone organises the competition. He also arranges all the torch-races. In fact he organises virtually all the traditional festivals.
>
> (*For the Lenaea, see CA 301–3*)

CA 221 ISOCRATES 7.29–30

> 29   To take first, as is proper, our forebears' dealing with the gods, there was nothing irregular or undisciplined about their worship and rites. They did not, if the whim took them, send 300 oxen for sacrifice and then perhaps omit altogether some traditional sacrifice: they did not celebrate magnificently new festivals involving a banquet and then pay for sacrifices on the
>
> 30   most venerable of holy days with the rent-money or by contract. Their sole concern was not to disturb tradition or to make extraordinary additions: reverence for the gods, they thought, consisted not in displays of extravagance but in this preservation of tradition. And, let me say, the answering action from the gods was correspondingly free from disturbing upsets, coming seasonably for the tilling of the earth and the gathering of the crops

CA 222 ISOCRATES 5.117

> In case of the gods too, those who bring us good are called Olympians, whereas those who control disasters and punishments have less pleasant

names. The former have altars and temples dedicated to them by individuals and by cities: the latter are not honoured by prayer or sacrifice – we simply take steps to avert them.

State Festivals:

CA 223 PLUTARCH, *Theseus* 22.3–5

(When Theseus returned home from Crete, joy at his coming was tempered by grief at the death of his father Aegeus, who had killed himself thinking Theseus dead)

3   This is the reason traditionally given why at the Oschophoria the participants cry "*Eleleu! Iou Iou!*" during the libations. The first is the customary cry of urgency and triumph, the second an indication of shock
4   and confusion. After burying his father, Theseus paid his vow to Apollo on the seventh day of the month *Pyanepsiôn* – the day they returned safe
5   to the city ... On this occasion they carry the *Eiresiônê*, an olive branch wreathed with wool (like Theseus' suppliant staff), and filled out with all kind of first-fruits, to signify the end of dearth, as they sing: "*Eiresiônê* brings figs and rich loaves, and honey in the pot and oil for anointing, and undiluted wine in the cup to bring drunken sleep."

For further details, see H. W. Parke: *Festivals of the Athenians*, pp. 77–80.

CA 224 Scholiast on LUCIAN, *Prostitutes' Dialogue* 2.1

Thesmophoria: a festival of the Greeks embracing mysteries. It was conducted according to the mythical story of Corê being abducted by Pluto while picking flowers. At that time and place a swineherd called Eubouleus was grazing his pigs and these were swallowed up in the chasm with Corê. So in honour of Eubouleus, piglets are thrown into the chasms of Demeter and Corê. Women called "flute-girls", after purifying themselves for three days, draw up again the rotted remains of the pigs thrown into the "*megara*". They go down into the sanctuary and after bringing them up, put them on the altars. Any one who takes any of these remains and puts it into the ground with the seed, will have an abundant harvest.

They say that there are snakes down below around the chasms which eat most of what is thrown in; so a noise is made whenever the women draw them up or put the images back again, so that the snakes which they reckon to be guardians of the sanctuary may withdraw.

Another name for the same is Arrhetophoria, and this is performed on the same principle, for the sake of the germination of crops and the fertility of men. There too sacred objects are carried, made out of dough, representing snakes and the figures of men. And they also take fir-cones because of the fertility of the tree, and these are thrown into the sanctuaries called "*megara*" ...

That is the mythical explanation of the festival. Here now is the physical one: it is called the Thesmophoria because Demeter bears the name

Thesmophoros, by virtue of having laid down a law or Thesmos according to which men have to provide food for themselves, and work for it.
(*See Parke pp. 156–169*)

CA 225 PLUTARCH, *Moralia* 99a (*On Chance*)

(*Plutarch is discussing whether Chance plays a part in the work of the craftsman, and suggests that hard work is the main factor in success, quoting these lines, probably of Sophocles (fr. 760)*)

Come into the street all you craftsmen people who worship Erganê (= *Athena as patron of the crafts*), the grim-eyed daughter of Zeus, with sacred baskets duly set out.
(*This is a reference to the craft-festival of the Chalkeia*)

The Eleusinian Mysteries (see Parke pp. 55–72):

CA 226 ISOCRATES 4.28

When Demeter came to our land at the time of her wanderings after the rape of Persephone, her gracious favour to our ancestors was won by those services to her about which only initiates may hear; and she gave us two supreme gifts: crops, which prevent our living the life of wild beasts, and the holy rite, which brings its initiates fairer hopes about the end of life and about life as a whole.

CA 227 XENOPHON, *Hellenica* 6.3.6

(*At the peace negotiations in the Spartan Assembly in 371 the first Athenian speaker is Callias, the torch-bearer in the Mysteries*)

"It was most improper that we should ever have taken up arms against each other, seeing that the first foreigners to whom our ancestor Triptolemus is said to have revealed the holy Mysteries of Demeter and Corê, were Heracles, your founder, and your fellow-citizens the Dioscuri; and the first place on which he bestowed the seed of the fruit of Demeter was the Peloponnese."

CA 228 ARISTOPHANES, *Frogs* 444–459

CHORUS OF INITIATES: Go now round the sacred precinct of the Goddess and the flower-laden grove, playing with those who share in a festival dear to the gods; and I will go with the girls and women, to bear the holy torch where they celebrate the Goddess' rites all night through.

448   Let us go to the meadows, full of blooming roses, celebrating after our own fashion the fairest of choral dances which the bounteous Muses

454   compose. On us alone shines the blissful radiance of the sun, on us

initiates whose way with strangers and ordinary people was respectful and pious.

CA 229 SOPHOCLES, fr. 753

How thrice-blessed are those mortals who pass to Hades after seeing these mysteries; for to them alone is it given to have life there, but to others all is evil there.

CA 230 ARISTOPHANES, *Peace* 371–375

HERMES. Don't you know that Zeus has ordained death for anyone found digging up this Peace?

TRYGAEUS. Must I die then?

HERMES. Of course.

TRYGAEUS. Lend me three drachmas for a piglet then; I must become an initiate before I die.

The secret of what was revealed to the initiates was well kept. Our only direct evidence comes from the Christian Fathers, who were concerned to discredit it.

CA 231 HIPPOLYTUS, *Refutation of Heresies* 5.8.39

The Athenians celebrating the Eleusinian Mysteries displayed to the initiates the great and wonderful and most perfect mystic revelation there – a harvested ear of corn.

CA 232 CLEMENT OF ALEXANDRIA, *Protrepticus* 2.18

I will cite for you the very words of Orpheus so that you may have the originator of the mysteries as a witness to their shamelessness: "This said, Baubo drew aside her robes and revealed every part of her body, even her private parts. The child Iacchus was there and, laughing, began to caress her below her breasts. When the goddess saw it, she smiled in her heart, and took up the gleaming cup in which the potion (*kykeôn*) was." And this is the summary (*synthêma*) of the Eleusinian Mysteries: "I fasted, I drank the potion, I took from the chest, I performed the actions, and put into the basket, and from the basket into the chest." Fine sights fit for a goddess! Rites worthy of darkness, fire and a hero, rather than the cunning people of Athens, let alone other Greeks for whom such things wait after death as they do not expect.

(*Baubo was the name of one of the aboriginal inhabitants of Eleusis, who offered hospitality to Demeter*)

CA 233 *SIG* 88.1–15, 25–33

(*Records of the Cult of Asclepius*)

1–15 The returning god was escorted to the temple of Eleusis with the Great Mysteries, and after sending for a snake from his home (*Epidaurus*), he brought this in a chariot. Telemachus met him, and at the same time came Hygieia (*Health*), and thus was founded the whole shrine in the archonship of Astyphilos (*420/19*).

25–33 Tisander: in his year (*414/3*) the wooden gateways were set up and the rest of the sacred building added.

Cleocritus: in his year (*413/2*) the whole sanctuary was planted and beautified at his own expense.

For details of the cult, see E. and L. Edelstein: *Asclepius*, vol. II. pp. 181–213; W.K.C. Guthrie: *The Greeks and their Gods* pp. 242–253.

Rituals based on the deme:

The following document prescribes details of sacrifices for the deme of Erchia, probably in the late 4th. century. For full analysis and interpretation, see the article by Sterling Dow in *BCH* 1965, pp. 180–213. The extract shows the requirements for the month Metageitniôn (= August).

CA 234 *The Greater Dêmarchia*

A 1–5	Metageitniôn: on the 12th, to Apollo Lykeios, in the City, a sheep, no removal: 12 dr.
B 1–5	on the 12th, in (the shrine of) Eleusis in the City, to Demeter, a sheep: 10 dr.
C 13–18	on the 12th, to Zeus Polieus, on the Acropolis in the City, a sheep, no removal, 12 dr.
D 13–17	on the 12th, to Athena Polias, on the Acropolis in the City, a sheep: 10 dr.
B 6–13	on the 16th, to the Nursing Mother, on the (altar) of Hecate at Erchia, a pig: 3 dr.; to Artemis Hecate, at Erchia, a goat: 10 dr.
E 1–8	on the 19th, to the Heroines, in the Reed-bed at Erchia, a sheep, no removal, the hide to the priestess: 10 dr.
A 6–11	on the 20th, to Hera Thelchinia, on the crag at Erchia, a ewe black all over, no removal: 7 dr.
C 19–25	on the 25th, to Zeus Epôpetês on the crag at Erchia, a pig, burnt whole without wine: 3 dr.

(*The phrase 'no removal' is taken to mean that the celebrant was not allowed to take away the meat*)

CA 235 *SIG* 921.10–25

(*Decree of the Attic phratry of the Demotionidae*)

This was decided by the phratry in the year when Phormio was archon at Athens (*396/5*) and Pantocles from Oeus was phratriarch . . .: Anyone who seems to have been introduced without being a member of the phratry, let the priest and phratriarch expunge his name from the register of the Demotionidae and from the copy. And let the person who introduced the disqualified man forfeit 100 dr. to Zeus of the Phratry.

Family religion:

CA 236 PLATO, *Euthydemus* 302b–d

"Tell me, Socrates" he said "Have you a hereditary Zeus?"

And I, foreseeing where the argument was heading, wriggled helplessly and tried to escape from the net. "No, Dionysiodorus" I said.

c　　　"Well, you're a miserable specimen of a man and not even an Athenian, if you have no hereditary gods or rites or any other such excellent thing."

"Please, Dionysiodorus, keep quiet and don't upbraid me. I do have altars and household and hereditary rites and others like those of the rest of the Athenians".

"Then haven't other Athenians a hereditary Zeus?" he asked.

d "No Ionian uses this title," I said, "neither colonists nor ourselves; we talk of a hereditary Apollo, because of the birth of Ion. Among us Zeus is called not hereditary but 'Zeus of the forecourt' or 'Zeus of the Phratriae', and Athena is called 'Athena of the Phratriae'."

"All right" he said. "So you have an Apollo and a Zeus and an Athena".

CA 237 DEMOSTHENES 43.57–58

(Quotation of Laws)

If a man dies in a deme and no one collects his body for burial, the demarch shall order the appropriate person to collect the body and bury it
58 and purify the deme on the day the man dies. In the case of slaves the order shall be given to the master: in the case of free men to whoever has the dead man's money: if he had no money, to his relations. If after the demarch's order the appropriate persons do not collect the body, the demarch shall contract for the collection and burial and the purification of the deme that same day as cheaply as possible; if the demarch does not so contract, he shall owe 1000 dr. to the treasury. He shall exact double whatever he spends from those properly responsible: if he fails to exact this, he shall himself owe the sum to his demesmen.

Those who do not pay their rent on the sacred precincts of the Goddess or other gods or the heroes shall lose all citizen-rights, themselves, their family and their heirs, until they pay.

CA 238 AELIAN, *Varied History* 5.14

This was also an Attic custom: anyone who came across the corpse of a man unburied was to throw earth on it without more ado, and bury it facing the sunset.

Private prayer and sacrifice:

CA 239 HIPPOCRATES, *Diet* 4.89

(From the section on dreams, where the author says that dreams of temperate weather conditions indicate a healthy body, and dreams of storms the opposite)

With this knowledge about the heavenly bodies then, one ought to take thought and change one's diet and pray to the gods – in the event of good signs to the Sun, to Heavenly Zeus and Zeus Ktesios (*the Protector*), to Athena Ktesia, to Hermes and Apollo; and if the signs are bad, to pray to the Averting deities, and to Earth and the Heroes, that all bad things may be averted.

CA 240 SOPHOCLES, *Oedipus Tyrannus* 158–167

CHORUS OF THEBAN ELDERS. First I call upon you, daughter of Zeus, immortal Athena, and Artemis guardian of the city, the Fair-famed one sitting on your throne in the agora, and brother Apollo the far-shooter. O three saviours, appear to me! If ever before to avert destruction rushing upon the city you have driven away the flame of evil, come now also.

CA 241 XENOPHON, *Anabasis* 7.8.4–5

(*Xenophon is told by the seer Euclides that there is something preventing him from acquiring more money*)

4   "It is Zeus the Gracious who is stopping you. Have you yet sacrificed to him, as I used to sacrifice for you, with whole burnt-offerings?"

Xenophon admitted that he had not sacrificed to this particular god ever since he had left home. Euclides advised him to sacrifice in the

5   customary way; it would be to his advantage, he said. On the next day Xenophon came to Ophrynium, and sacrificed according to ancient usage, burning whole pigs. The omens proved favourable.

CA 242 ANTIPHON 1.16, 18–19

16   After this it so happened that Philoneus had a sacrifice to make to Zeus Ktesios in Piraeus and my father was about to sail to Naxos. So Philoneus decided on one and the same journey to escort my father, a friend of his, to

18   Piraeus and after making his sacrifice to entertain him to a meal.... When they had dined, as you would expect, since one was sacrificing to Zeus Ktesios and entertaining his friend and the other was about to sail and being entertained to dinner, they made libations and put frankincense on

19   the altar for their own safety and prosperity. But Philoneus' mistress was pouring the libation as they prayed – prayers not destined to fulfilment, gentlemen – and she poured in the poison.

CA 243 APOLLONIUS OF RHODES, *Argonautica* 3.1027–1036

(*Medea's instructions to Jason for making a sacrifice to Hecate*)

When you meet my father and he gives you the dread dragon's teeth for

1030 you to sow, you must wait for the very middle of the night, and then, after bathing in the waters of a perennial river, you must put on dark clothes, and all alone dig a round pit, and slaughter a ewe in it and sacrifice it

1035 whole, after heaping up a fine pyre over the pit; and pour a libation of honey from the hive, and pray to Hecate, only daughter of Perses.

CA 244 AESCHYLUS, *Choephori* 124–149

(*Electra prays at the tomb of her father Agamemnon*)

Mighty herald of those above and below, Chthonic Hermes, help me. Tell the deities below the earth who watch over my father's house to hear my

130 prayers.... As for me it is to a mortal that I pour this libation, as I call upon my father saying: "Have pity upon me and dear Orestes.... I pray

140 to you that by some chance Orestes may come here; and for me myself grant that my actions may be much more restrained and pious than those of my mother. This I pray for us, and for our enemies that one may appear to avenge you, father, and that your killers may justly perish in their

turn.... May you escort these blessings up to us from the underworld, together with the gods and earth and justice, bearer of victory."

Worship of non-Olympian deities:

CA 245 *IG* I² 784–5, 788

Inscriptions found in a cave near Anagyrus (date uncertain).

784 Archidamus of Thera planted this garden for the Nymphs.
785 Archidamus of Thera also built a dancing-place for the Nymphs.
788 Archidamus of Thera, driven wild by the Nymphs (*lit. nymphstruck*) fashioned this cave at the prompting of the Nymphs.

In Euripides, *Electra* 783–807 Aegisthus is sacrificing to the Nymphs when struck down by Orestes.

CA 246 CICERO, *On the Laws* 2.37

(*In a passage concerning the need to restrict initiatory rites of a suspicious character*)

Aristophanes, the wittiest poet of ancient comedy, attacks new deities and worship that required nocturnal vigils, to the point of having Sabazius and some of the other foreign deities brought to trial and expelled from the state.
     (*The work of Aristophanes referred to is no longer extant*)

CA 247 JUVENAL 2.91–92, with Scholiast

(*From a passage describing secret transvestite rituals at Rome*)

Such orgiastic rites were celebrated by torchlight when the Baptae used to exhaust Athenian Cottyto.
     Scholiast: "*Baptae*" is the name of a work by Eupolis describing the disgraceful behaviour of transvestite Athenians who danced until the music-girl was exhausted. So Baptae were effeminates who gave their name to a comedy of Eupolis, which led to his death at the hands of Alcibiades who was one of his principal targets.

CA 248 DEMOSTHENES 18.259–260

259 When you (Aeschines) came to manhood, you used to read out the service books to your mother when she officiated at initiations and in other ways acted as her assistant, at night dressing the initiates in fawn-skins and drenching them in wine and cleansing them and smearing them with the mud and bran treatment, then raising them from the purification ceremony as you bid them chant "Farewell to the bad, all hail to the better", priding yourself that no one had ever cried it louder (and I can well believe it: you would not expect a man with such a loud voice not to be an
260 outstanding crier); and by day leading splendid routs through the streets of men garlanded in fennel and poplar, and whacking the fat-cheeked

snakes and whirling them round your head, and shouting "*Euoi Saboi*"
and dancing the "*Hyes Attes, Attes Hyes*" as chorus leader, bearer of the
ivy and the winnowing-fan, (and so addressed by the hags,) taking as your
fee sops, and twists and barley-buns – a splendid life indeed!

Orphism:

CA 249 PLATO, *Cratylus* **400b–c**

b   (HERMOGENES. What about the word "*sôma*" for the body?)

c   SOCRATES. Some people say the body is the tomb (*sêma*) of the soul which
        is for the time being buried in it; and they also think "*sêma*" is the right
        word because the soul gives all its signals (*sêmainei*) by means of the
        body. I think it was above all Orpheus' circle who applied the word
        "*sôma*" on the grounds that the soul is undergoing punishment for
        whatever reason and has a prison-wall in the form of the body to keep it
        in (*sôsdein*); and so, they say, the body, as its name implies, is a keep
        ("*sôma*") for the soul until it has paid its due penalty, and there is no
        need to alter a single letter of the word.

(b) Belief in Divine Power (CA 250–273)

The performance of all this ritual presupposes a belief in the ability of the gods
to intervene in human affairs; the purpose of prayer and sacrifice is to enlist this
divine power on one's own side, or to avert its potential hostility. Although
there was plenty of scepticism to be found in Athens at this time, it figures with
undue prominence in the sources, most of which emanated from the intellectual
minority. The majority of Athenians probably continued to hold orthodox
views simply because their fathers had done so, and nowhere are these views
more clearly expressed than in Herodotus. He says (9.100) that "there is plenty
of evidence to show the hand of the gods in ordering human affairs"; this
manifests itself in the belief that wickedness is punished (that for instance is
Herodotus' explanation for the destruction of Troy, 2.120), and virtue re-
warded. Another orthodox believer was Nicias: when the Athenian expedition
to Sicily was on the brink of final disaster, he exhorts his troops to trust that the
gods will now be on their side because of his own exemplary piety, and because
their own sufferings and the successes of the enemy have reached their limit
(Thuc. 7.77.1–4)

   Allied to this idea of the divine ordering of things is the belief that the ways of
the gods may be made known to man through the medium of oracles,
prophecies, portents and dreams. All figure prominently in 5th.-century drama.
Herodotus again firmly asserts his belief in the efficacy of oracles (8.77) and the
likelihood of impending good and ill being foreshadowed by portents (6.27).
Most ordinary people shared these beliefs: when the dramatic eclipse of the
moon occurred on 27 August 413, it was not just Nicias who wanted to
postpone the Athenian departure from Syracuse, but "the majority of the
soldiers urged the generals to wait" (Thuc.7.50.7).

   The meaning of these revelations of the divine will was not often immediately
clear to the recipient; they required interpreters with special skills. So there grew

up a class of professional oracle-mongers and fortune-tellers, many of them no doubt charlatans whose only aim was to exploit the credulity of others.

CA 250 XENOPHON, *Memorabilia* 4.3.15–16

15   Euthydemus said: "I am sure, Socrates, that I shall be punctilious in my relations with the deity; but I am depressed by the thought that no mortal could ever thank the gods enough for their services."

16   "Cheer up, Euthydemus, and remember that when the god at Delphi is asked how one can find favour with the gods, he answers 'Do what everyone else in the state does'. And what everyone else does, I suppose, is to try and please the gods with sacrifices as best he can."

CA 251 SOPHOCLES, *Oedipus Tyrannus* 863–872

CHORUS OF THEBAN ELDERS. May it be my destiny to find reverent purity of words and actions, such as are sanctioned by the sublime laws, created in the heavens; Olympus is their sole father, and no mortal nature of men created them, nor ever shall they be laid to rest in oblivion. God is great in these things and ages not.
(*See also Sophocles' Antigone 450–457*)

CA 252 LYSIAS 6.10

Yet they say Pericles once urged you in dealing with the impious not to employ only the written laws but also the unwritten, which the Eumolpidae use for their pronouncements and which no one yet has had the power to destroy or the nerve to oppose, nor has anyone known their author; the impious, he said, would then realise they were being punished by the gods as well as by men.

CA 253 PLATO, *Laws* 793a–c

All the laws we are now discussing are those commonly known as
b   unwritten laws and in fact all hereditary customs come under this head. And we were quite right in making our recent proviso that we should neither call them laws nor on the other hand leave them unmentioned; for they are the bonds of every society, linking together all written laws past, present and future, – hereditary and utterly ancient customs, which, if they are soundly established, hold together in a mantle of absolute security all
c   subsequent written laws; but, if they go away, like joiners' supports in buildings when they give way from the middle, bring everything else to the ground with them on top of each other; and there they lie both themselves and later additions however well built, because the original supports have collapsed.

CA 254 PAUSANIAS 10.28. 5–6

In Polygnotus' painting, near the man who injured his father and is for that reason suffering torment in Hades, a man who has pillaged sanctuaries is punished. The woman who is punishing him is expert in drugs,
6   especially ones painful to people. People were, you understand, still immensely devoted to religion, as the Athenians showed when they captured a sanctuary of Olympian Zeus at Syracuse, without disturbing

any of the dedications, and leaving the Syracusan priest to look after them. . . . Thus at that time everyone held the gods in honour, and on that basis Polygnotus painted the section relating to the temple-robber.

CA 255 LYSIAS fr. 53

I am surprised that you are not angry at the idea of Cinesias being an upholder of the law, when you all know that he is the most unprincipled law-breaker ever. Is it not he that committed such outrages concerning the gods as others would be ashamed to speak of even, though they are the regular fare of the comic poets? Did he not once have a party with Apollophanes, Mystalides and Lysitheus, choosing one of the ill-omened days, and calling themselves not New-Mooners but the Hellfire Club (*kakodaimonistai*) – an appropriate name in view of their fate; not that this was their intention; they were simply making fun of the gods and your laws. Each one of them died, as you would expect. But this was the treatment reserved by the gods for Cinesias, the best known of them: his enemies preferred him not to die, but to stay alive as an example to others that when people commit the most wanton outrages against religion, punishment is not always put off onto their children, but they themselves are miserably destroyed as ever greater and harsher disasters and diseases are heaped upon them, more than upon the rest of mankind.

(*The notion of children inheriting their fathers' guilt occurs in other writers of the period, notably Herodotus, e.g. 7.134–7*)

CA 256 ANDOCIDES 1.137–139

137 They also attacked me on the subject of my acts as a ship-owner and trader, making the absurd accusation that the gods had apparently preserved me from danger just so that I could be destroyed by Cephisius. Gentlemen, I scarcely think that if the gods thought they had been wronged by me, they would fail to have their revenge when they had caught me in the gravest of perils, the peril of being at sea in a winter storm: they had me at their mercy, life and property – and they let me

138 escape? Could they not have ensured me a watery grave without even
139 burial? . . . Can you really suppose that instead they appointed Cephisius as their avenger, Cephisius the biggest crook in Athens, . . . a man whom none of my audience would trust in any private matter, knowing him for what he is? In my view, gentlemen, perils such as mine now are man-made, while perils at sea come from the gods: and if I am to speculate on divine affairs, I imagine the gods would be very angry and upset if they saw those whom they themselves had saved destroyed by human agents.

CA 257 PLUTARCH, *Pericles* 13.7–8

7 The Propylaea on the Acropolis was built in five years; Mnesicles was the architect. A remarkable incident connected with the building showed that the goddess, far from dissociating herself from the work, was actually

8 helping it towards completion. The most energetic and keen of the workmen fell from high up and lay stricken, despaired of by the doctors. Pericles was despondent, but the goddess appeared to him in a dream and

prescribed a course of treatment which he followed; the man made a rapid and easy recovery. For this Pericles set up the bronze statue to Athena of Health on the Acropolis.

Oracles:

CA 258 XENOPHON, *Memorabilia* 1.1.3

(*Xenophon is dealing with the charge that Socrates "introduced new deities"*)

In fact he introduced nothing new, any more than the people who believe in divination, and make use of augury, oracles, omens and sacrifices. They do not suppose that the birds or the people they chance to meet know what is good for the oracle-seekers; rather that the gods use such things to indicate their intentions. That was what Socrates thought too.

CA 259 XENOPHON, *Memorabilia* 4.3.12

(*Euthydemus accepts Socrates' proposition that almost everything is made providentially for man's good*)

"Everything points to the conclusion that the gods take great care of man."

"And that they help us over our inability to see what is best for the future by using the medium of divination to reveal to the enquirer what will happen and what the best course of action is."

CA 260 PLATO, *Phaedrus* 244a–d

The prophetess at Delphi and the priestesses at Dodona have performed
b   many splendid services for Greece, both personal and public, when in a manic state; but when in their right mind they have done little or nothing. And there is no need to expatiate on the powers of the Sibyl and all others who have used mantic inspiration to foretell the future successfully to many people on many occasions. It is worth noting that in fact those who of old times gave names to things did not regard mania as anything
c   disgraceful or reprehensible; otherwise they would not have called the noblest art, that which foretells the future, the "manic" art, which involves the notion of mania. They gave the name on the assumption that it was a noble art whenever given divine support, and it is men of our own times who have stuck in a philistine 't' and called it the "mantic" art. And a similar thing has happened with the sober art of those who enquire into the future by means of birds (*ornithes*) and other signs: on the grounds that these signs were intended to provide human thought (*oiêsis*) with
d   sense (*nous*) and scientific knowledge (*historia*), people of old called this the "*oionoïstic*" art, and "*oiônistic*", with its portentous long 'ô', is only a recent neologism. Well, just as both in name and fact the mantic art is more valid and more valuable than the oionistic art, so the ancients bear witness that mania is something superior to sobriety, the one coming from god the other from man.

(*Dodona in Epirus housed an oracle of Zeus*)

CA 261 ARISTOPHANES, *Peace* 1052–1073

(*Trygaeus' sacrifice to Peace is interrupted by the arrival of Hierocles, the oracle-expounder*)

HIEROCLES. What sacrifice is this, and to which of the gods?

TRYGAEUS. Keep your mouth shut, carry on cooking, and you get away from the loin.

HIEROCLES. Will you not tell me to whom you are sacrificing?

TRYGAEUS. The tail's doing nicely.

1055 SLAVE. Yes, beautifully, dear Lady Peace.

HIEROCLES. Come now, begin, and give me the first cut.

TRYGAEUS. It needs roasting first.

HIEROCLES. It is roasted already.

TRYGAEUS. Stop interfering, whoever you are. (*To slave*) Keep on slicing. Where's the table? Bring the libation.

1060 HIEROCLES. The tongue should be cut out separately.

TRYGAEUS. I know. What you should do is . . .

HIEROCLES. Tell me.

TRYGAEUS. Stop interrupting us. We're sacrificing to Peace.

HIEROCLES. You poor foolish mortals . . .

TRYGAEUS. Same to you.

1064 HIEROCLES. . . . Who in your ignorance, not knowing the will of the gods
1070   have made a truce with those furious monkeys (= *Spartans*) . . . For unless Bakis has been deceived by the Nymphs, or mortals by Bakis, or again Bakis by the Nymphs . . .

TRYGAEUS. To hell with you, if you don't put a stop to this Baking.

HIEROCLES. Not yet is the bond of Peace destined to be loosed.

(*Bakis is the name given to several famous expounders of oracles*)

CA 262 PLUTARCH, *Nicias* 13.1–2, 5

1   And yet many objections are said to have been put forward by the priests. Alcibiades however had different soothsayers and presented certain sayings from ancient oracles, which declared that the Athenians would win great fame from Sicily. Certain messengers from Ammon arrived for him bringing an oracle to the effect that the Athenians would capture all the Syracusans. They suppressed the predictions to the contrary, fearing to speak words of ill omen, for not even clear and obvious signs served to
2   deter them. These were the mutilation of the Hermae, when they had their extremities cut off in one night – all that is except one which they call the Herm of Andocides . . .; and also the incident concerning the altar of the twelve gods: a man suddenly leapt onto it and castrated himself with a stone as he stood astride it.

    (*Other portents at Delphi are described*)

5   Either from fear of these events, or because his human reasoning made him fear the expedition, the astrologer Meton, who had been appointed to some command, pretended to set fire to his house as if he had gone mad. Some however assert that he did not feign madness, but that he set fire to his house at night, and proceeded to the market-place and began to beg

the citizens to relieve his son of his command because of this great disaster. His son was about to sail to Sicily in the capacity of a trierarch.

CA 263 PAUSANIAS 8.11.12

The Athenians obtained an oracle from Dodona that they should settle in Sicily; this is a small hill not far from the city. But they without considering what had been said were led on to overseas campaigns and the war with Syracuse.

CA 264 *SIG* 73

Bronze plate from Dodona (?429)

The Athenians made this offering after defeating the Peloponnesians in a sea-battle.

CA 265 PLUTARCH, *Nicias* 4.1–2

1   Nicias was one of those deeply in awe of the supernatural, and as
2   Thucydides says, "heavily reliant on divination". In one of Pasiphon's dialogues we are told that he sacrificed daily to the gods, and kept a fortune-teller at his house, supposedly for consultations about state-business, but in fact mostly for his private affairs, in particular the silver-mines.

CA 266 ISOCRATES 19.5–6

5   Thrasyllus ... received no capital from his forebears but became a friend of Polemaenetus, the prophet, – such a close friend that on his death bed Polemaenetus left him his books on prophecy and part of his present
6   capital. On acquiring these sources of income, he set about practising the trade as an itinerant ...
   (cf. Aristides' grandson (CA 87))

Dreams and portents:

CA 267 XENOPHON, *Anabasis* 3.1.11–12

(Xenophon is worried about the implications of joining Cyrus' expedition against the Persian King)

11   Xenophon was as worried as everyone else and unable to sleep. When he did manage to doze off for a bit, he had a dream: there was a clap of thunder, and lightning fell on his father's house, setting the whole place
12   alight. At once he woke up in a panic. In one way the dream seemed good, because in the midst of his troubles and dangers he seemed to have seen a great light from Zeus; on the other hand he was afraid because the fact that the dream seemed to come from Zeus the King, and that the fire seemed to blaze all around, might mean that he would be unable to get out of the country of the Great King because of the difficulties pressing in on him from every side.

(After a while Xenophon decides not just to sit and wait for his destiny to be fulfilled, but to take the initiative and trust to his own resources to keep him from danger)

CA 268 XENOPHON, *Anabasis* 6.1.22–23

(Xenophon is trying to decide whether to accept sole command of the army)

22 As he was still quite unable to make up his mind, he thought it best to consult the gods; and setting up two altars he sacrificed to Zeus the King – who was the god recommended to him by the Delphic oracle, and from whom he thought his dream had come when he took the first step towards
23 a share in the command of the army. He also remembered that when he was leaving Ephesus to go and be introduced to Cyrus, there was an eagle screaming on his right – a sitting one, it is true; the soothsayer who was escorting him said that this was no ordinary omen, but indicated greatness and glory, albeit hard-won; for birds are most likely to attack an eagle when it is sitting.

CA 269 XENOPHON, *Anabasis* 3.2.8–9

(Xenophon addresses his men before a battle)

8   "If we resolve to make total war on the enemy henceforward, we have,
9   with the god's help, many fair hopes of salvation." Just as he was saying this, a man sneezed. When the soldiers heard it, they bowed to the god with a single impulse; and Xenophon said: "Since an omen from Zeus the Saviour has been revealed to us at the moment the word 'salvation' was mentioned, I think we ought to vow to that god to sacrifice thank-offerings for salvation as soon as we reach friendly territory; and further sacrifices to the rest of the gods, in so far as we are able."

CA 270 THEOPHRASTUS, *Characters* 16.7–8, 11–12

The superstitious man.

7   He makes a great palaver of purifying his house, saying that Hecate has put it under a spell. And if owls hoot as he is out walking, he is deeply perturbed and says "Athena is greater" before passing on . . .
11 . . . Whenever he has a dream he goes to the interpreters of dreams, the
12 seers or diviners, to ask which god or goddess he ought to pray to; and when he is going to be initiated, he goes to the priests of Orpheus each month along with his wife – or if his wife is too busy, with the nurse – and his children.

CA 271 PLUTARCH, *Pericles* 38.2

(In 429 Pericles succumbed to the Plague, not in its most virulent form, but one which had a protracted debilitating effect)

Theophrastus in his *Ethics* (which questions whether character is modified by events and compelled by bodily sufferings to abandon excellence) records that when Pericles was ill he showed to a visiting friend an amulet tied round his neck by the womenfolk, implying that he must be in a really bad way to put up with nonsense like that.

Witchcraft:

CA 272 ARISTOPHANES, *Clouds* 747–756

STREPSIADES. I've got an idea for getting rid of interest.
SOCRATES. Let's have it.
STREPSIADES. Tell me now . . .
SOCRATES. What?
749 STREPSIADES. Suppose I paid a Thessalian witch to spirit away the moon in the middle of the night, and then I stowed it away in a round box, like a mirror, and kept watch over it.
SOCRATES. What good would that do you?
755 STREPSIADES. Well, if the moon never rose again, I wouldn't have to repay any interest.
SOCRATES. Why should that be?
STREPSIADES. Because interest is lent by the month.

CA 273 PLATO, *Laws* 933a–b

a   The other (psychological) form of drugging is that which by quackeries and incantations and so-called spells convinces those who are prepared to do harm that they have the power to do so and convinces their intended victims that the power of such charms can harm them more than anything else. It is not easy to discover the scientific truth in this whole sphere nor to persuade others of it, once discovered; when men are mentally out of
b   countenance with each other, it is not worth trying to persuade them that, if they happen to see wax images somewhere, on doors or at cross-roads or perhaps on their parents' tombs, they should urge anyone who has no clear understanding of these matters to make light of them.

(c) Rationalism and Scepticism (CA 274–297)

The views of those influenced by the new sophistic teaching are well represented by Thucydides. He ascribes natural causes to phenomena like eclipses (2.28), and is sceptical about oracles (2.54) and divine providence: prayers for divine aid are invariably futile (the Athenians at the time of the plague, 2.47.4; the people of Melos, 5.104,112; and Nicias, p. 92). Similar ideas are found in the medical writers and the works of Euripides (though one must be wary of ascribing to the author the views of all his characters), as well as the sophists themselves. Their main contentions are that traditional beliefs in the gods afford no adequate basis for morality, and that in any case knowledge of the nature and indeed existence of the gods is impossible. One view that found its way into popular thought equated God with Air. Purely atheistic attitudes were not commonly adopted, though there were certainly some who professed a thoroughgoing scepticism about the supernatural. The state did its best to maintain the status of orthodoxy; criminal proceedings for impiety were not uncommon, though there was often some political motive underlying the prosecution. Thucydides cannot have been alone in thinking that when in the face of disaster the old system of beliefs broke down (as during the plague, 2.53; and the Corcyran revolution, 3.82), the catastrophe was compounded.

CA 274 EURIPIDES, *Helen* 1137–1150

What is god or not god or in between, what mortal can say that he has discovered, though he search to the furthest limits, seeing the divine will leaping this way and that and back again by chance inexplicable, unhoped-for? . . . I cannot say that anything among mortals is sure; but the word of God I have found to be unerring.

CA 275 EURIPIDES, Hippolytus 1102–1117

1102 CHORUS (*identity uncertain*). When I think of the gods' care for men, my anxieties are lifted; but while harbouring some hopes of understanding, I am baffled when I look upon the fortunes and actions of men. One change follows another, and the life of man is never stable, ever
1111 wandering. May the gods grant me this destiny in answer to my prayer: fortune with prosperity, and a mind untroubled by ills. May my thoughts not be rigid, nor again counterfeit, my sentiments changing easily as the morrow requires, joining in the good fortune of life.

CA 276 EURIPIDES, *Trojan Women* 884–889

HECUBA. O upholder of the earth, enthroned over the earth, O beyond comprehension, whoever you be, O Zeus, a compelling law of nature or the mind of man, to you I pray; for treading a noiseless path, you direct the affairs of men according to justice.
MENELAUS. What's all that? A novel prayer to the gods you've made.

CA 277 EURIPIDES, *Heracles* 1341–1346

HERACLES. I do not believe that the gods approve of unlawful sex; I have never thought, nor will I be persuaded that a god may be fettered or lord it over another. For God, if he is truly God, needs nothing. Those are but the wretched stories of minstrels.

CA 278 EURIPIDES, *Bellerophon* (fr. 292)

Of the diseases of mankind, some are self-inflicted, others come from the gods, but we treat them by conventional means. But I suggest to you that if the gods do anything reprehensible, they are not gods.

CA 279 DIOGENES LAERTIUS 9.51–52

Protagoras was the first to say that there were two arguments opposed to one another on every topic: with these he would put a series of questions, the first to do this. However, he also started in this way: "Man is the measure of all things, of what exists that it is, and of what does not exist that it is not." He also said that the soul was nothing by comparison with the senses, just as Plato says in the *Theaetetus*, and that everything was true. Elsewhere he started like this: "About the gods I am unable to know either that they exist, or that they do not; for there are many obstacles to knowledge, the obscurity of the subject and the brevity of human life." It was because of this start to his book that he was expelled by the Athenians, who burnt his books in the market-place, after collecting them up from each of the owners under a herald's supervision.

52

He was the first to charge a fee, 100 minas; he first divided up periods of time, expounded the power of opportunity and established debates and introduced verbal tricks to people engaged in argument; he abandoned the sense and addressed himself to the letter of the word and created the present shallow type of sophistry; where Timon says of him:

"Protagoras the good mixer, the expert debater."

(*On Protagoras, see Index*)

CA 280 PLUTARCH, *Pericles* 6.1–2

1   It was not only these benefits which Pericles derived from his association with Anaxagoras, but he also seems to have risen above all superstition which is produced, in those who do not know the causes of such

2   manifestations, by amazement at heavenly phenomena ... It is said that once the head of a one-horned ram was brought to Pericles from the country, and that Lampon the seer, when he saw that the horn had grown strong and solid from the middle of the forehead, said that there were two areas of power in the city, that of Thucydides (*son of Melesias*) and that of Pericles; and that supremacy would devolve upon whichever of them was given the portent. Anaxagoras however had the skull split open, and showed that the brain had not fully developed in the skull cavity, but tapered like an egg and extended only to that area where the root of the horn began.

(*On Anaxagoras, see Index*)

CA 281 ANTIPHON (*Sophist*) fr. 9

When Antiphon was asked what prophecy was, he said: "A guess by a sensible man".

CA 282 HIPPOCRATES, *Sacred Disease* 1

On the Sacred Disease: this disease does not seem to me to be more sacred and divine than any other, but has its own nature and cause. And it is only men's inexperience and bewilderment at its peculiarities that make them regard it as sacred. So long as this ignorance persists, its "sacredness" is perpetuated; but this is undermined by their readiness to adopt methods of cure like purifications and incantations. But if it is to be thought sacred just because it is remarkable, then there should be not just one Sacred Disease but many, as I can show other diseases no less remarkable and wondrous, which however no one considers sacred.

CA 283 DIOGENES fr. 5

It seems to me that the thing that has understanding is what is called "air" by man, and this is what governs and controls everyone. In fact this very thing seems to me to be a god, and to reach everything and arrange everything and be in everything.

CA 284 PHILEMON fr. 91

He whose eye misses nothing, whatever anyone does or will do or has done in the past, yet is neither god nor man, I am he – Air, though some might call me Zeus. I am everywhere – the characteristic of a god – here in Athens, in Patras, in Sicily, in every city, in every house, among you all. There is no place where Air is not. And he who is everywhere must know everything.

CA 285 ARISTOPHANES, *Clouds* 264–266

SOCRATES (*invoking the Chorus of Clouds*). O Lord and Master, measure-less Air who upholds the Earth in mid-universe, and bright Ether, and Clouds, awesome goddesses of thunder and lightning, rise and appear in our midst.

CA 286 ARISTOPHANES, *Clouds* 365–381

SOCRATES. These clouds are the only goddesses, and all the rest are just rubbish.
STREPSIADES. But by Earth, do you not regard Olympian Zeus as a god?
SOCRATES. Zeus? Don't talk nonsense. He doesn't even exist.
STREPSIADES. What's that you say? Who makes the rain? Tell me that first.
SOCRATES. The clouds do of course. I'll show you. The evidence is clear.
370   Come now, have you ever seen it raining without clouds? Conversely you would expect it to rain from a clear sky, with no clouds in sight.
STREPSIADES. By Apollo, you've grafted that well onto our argument. And before this, I always thought it was Zeus peeing through a sieve. But tell me, who makes the thunder that I'm so frightened of?
375 SOCRATES. It's only the clouds rolling along.
STREPSIADES. What a monstrous idea! How?
SOCRATES. When they are filled with a lot of water and are set in motion, and the weight of rain makes them hang down of necessity, then as they clash heavily against each other, they crack and burst.
STREPSIADES. But isn't it Zeus who provides the necessity that sets them in motion?

380 SOCRATES. Not at all, but the *Dinos* (vortex) of Ether.

STREPSIADES. *Dinos*? I had no idea that Zeus didn't exist, and *Dinos* was now reigning in his place.

CA 287 *IG* I.² 945

From the funerary monument to those Athenians who died at the siege of Potidaea (432–1)

Ether received the souls and (earth) the bodies of these men.

CA 288 THRASYMACHUS fr. 8

In his own work he wrote something to the effect that the gods do not see men's deeds. They would not have disregarded the greatest good among men, which is justice. We see that men do not practise this virtue.

CA 289 XENOPHON, *Memorabilia* 1.4.10–11

10 Aristodemus said: "I certainly don't despise the deity, Socrates; but I reckon it too high and mighty to need my attention."

"But in that case, if something high and mighty deigns to pay attention to you, you ought to pay it all the more respect."

11 "Believe me, I wouldn't neglect the gods if I thought that they paid any heed to man."

CA 290 CICERO, *On the Nature of the Gods* 3.89

When Diagoras, who was called the Atheist, came to Samothrace, a friend said to him: "You think that the gods are heedless of human affairs, but don't you see, on the evidence of the numerous votive tablets, how many people have by their prayers escaped the violence of the storm and reached harbour safely?"

He replied, "That's because there are no painted tablets of those who have suffered shipwreck and perished in the sea."

CA 291 SEXTUS EMPIRICUS, *Against the Teachers* 1.53–54

53 And Diagoras the dithyrambic poet was to begin with, so they say, as god-fearing as the next man; in fact he began his poem like this: "Everything is done according to divine will and chance (or, fortune)." But when he was wronged by a man who broke his oath and got away with it, he changed to
54 saying that God did not exist. And Critias, one of the Thirty Tyrants at Athens, seems to belong to the ranks of the atheists, saying that the ancients invented God to act as a sort of superviser of man's good and bad conduct, so that fear of divine vengeance might discourage anyone from harming his neighbour secretly.

Then follows a long quotation from Critias' lost play *Sisyphus* (fr. 1) setting out this theory of divinity at greater length. A translation of most of the passage may be found on pp. 243–4 of W. K. C. Guthrie: *The Sophists*.

CA 292 CICERO, *On the Nature of the Gods* 1.32

Antisthenes, in the book entitled *The Natural Scientist*, says that there are numerous gods in popular belief, but only one in nature, thus removing from the gods their power and character.

CA 293 DIOGENES LAERTIUS 6.2,4

2   (Antisthenes) His home was at Piraeus, but each day he went up the seven miles and listened to Socrates . . .

4   . . . Once when being initiated in Orphic ritual, as the priest stated that those who underwent this initiation shared in many blessings in Hades, he said "Why don't you die, then?"

CA 294 SEXTUS EMPIRICUS, *Against the Teachers* 1.18

Prodicus of Ceos says: "The ancients reckoned as gods the sun and moon and rivers and springs and in general everything that helps our lives, because of the help we get from them – just as the Egyptians regard the Nile."

Religion and the state:

CA 295 PLUTARCH, *Nicias* 23.2–3

2   The majority thought that the eclipse of the sun around the thirtieth of the month was due to the moon. As for the moon however, it was not easy to understand what object it encountered, and how the light disappeared and blazed forth in manifold splendour from a full moon. They thought it was strange, and that a sign from god was being revealed heralding some great disasters. For Anaxagoras, the first man to commit to writing the clearest and boldest of all the accounts of the radiance and overshadowing of the moon was neither long-established himself nor did his account enjoy any reputation – it was still secret and was being passed on with caution rather

3   than conviction among very few hands. People were intolerant of natural scientists and so-called "star-gazers", because they reduced Providence to irrational causes and random powers and necessary effects; in fact Protagoras was exiled, Anaxagoras was imprisoned and only just rescued by Pericles, and Socrates was executed because of philosophy, even though he had nothing to do with such things.
     (*See also CA 172, and for the trial of Socrates CA 437–449*)

CA 296 PLUTARCH, *Alcibiades* 19.1–2

1   At this point the popular leader Androcles produced some slaves and metics who accused Alcibiades and his friends of disfiguring other statues, and of parodying the Mysteries when drunk. They said that one Theodorus played the part of the Herald, Pulytion that of the Torch-bearer, and Alcibiades that of the Hierophant; and that the rest of his companions were there and took part in the Mystery rites under the name of Mystae.

2   These were the charges in the indictment (*eisangelia*) when Alcibiades was publicly indicted for impiety by Thessalus son of Cimon.

CA 297 PLUTARCH, *Alcibiades* 20.2–4

2   To begin with, as I have said, Alcibiades only faced a few mild suspicions
3   and slanders from slaves and metics. But once he had left Athens, his enemies attacked more vehemently, and suggested that the outrages against the Hermae and the Mysteries were implicated with a revolutionary conspiracy; they threw into prison without trial anyone who had been charged in any way, and were angry that they had not subjected Alcibiades to legal process and judgement at the time, when the charges
4   were so grave. Their anger against him extended to any member of his household, and friend or acquaintance, and they were liable to be harshly treated.

(*For the Hermae affair, see also Thuc. 6.27–29, 53,61, and CA 66, 150*)

VI. THE ARTS

(a) The Dramatic Festivals (CA 298–318)

Dionysus was the patron god of drama, and two of the Athenian festivals held in his honour – the Lenaea and the City Dionysia – were marked by competitions for tragedy and comedy. To these should also be added a third, the Rural Dionysia, which had started as a simple country festival (parodied in Aristophanes, *Acharnians* 241–279), but had been upgraded to include performances by touring dramatic companies as other towns in Attica started building their own theatres.

The Lenaea – a name taken nowadays to refer to the Lenai, or ecstatic devotees of Dionysus – was a winter festival, exclusive to Athenians, at which there was a competition for comedies. To judge from the plays of Aristophanes produced at it, it must have acquired a prestige in comedy comparable with that of the main Dionysiac festival.

The City Dionysia in the spring was a big enough occasion to be used for international business (like the renewal of the alliance between Athens and Sparta signed in 421, Thuc.5.23.4) as well as providing prolonged public entertainment for everyone; it lasted a full week, and even the gaols were emptied. Onto the original Dionysiac ritual – the bringing of the god's statue into the city, the procession, and the revel (*kômos*) – was grafted the apparatus of a major dramatic competition. There were prizes for choruses, actors and playwrights in the performance of dithyrambs (choral lyrics), tragedy and comedy. At the start of the year the Eponymous Archon appointed *chorêgi*, selected writers, and allocated lead-actors. The *chorêgus* was responsible for the training and fitting out of a chorus, and had a good opportunity for self-advertisement by lavish spending on costumes (see CA 28). The drama contests involved three writers of tragedy (each putting on a "trilogy" of three plays, not necessarily related in theme, and a satyr play as a finale); and five of comedy (though the number was reduced to three during the Peloponnesian War for economy reasons). Audiences were given a foretaste of the plays in the *Proagôn*, where excerpts were shown in Pericles' Odeum by the actors without their masks on. This would help the audience to identify them in the actual performance, where popular applause undoubtedly helped to sway the official judges in their verdict.

Besides the standard work – A. W. Pickard-Cambridge: *The Dramatic Festivals of Athens* – see also H. W. Parke: *Festivals of the Athenians*, pp. 100–106, 125–136.

CA 298 HESYCHIUS, under *Dionysia*

Festival of Dionysus at Athens; the Rural Dionysia was held in the month of Posideôn (*Nov/Dec*), the Lenaea in the month of Gamêliôn (*Dec/Jan*), the City Dionysia in the month of Elaphêboliôn (*Feb/Mar*).

Rural Dionysia:

CA 299 ARISTOTLE, *Constitution of Athens* 54.8

They also appoint by lot an officer for Salamis and a demarch for Piraeus who arrange the Dionysia in each place and appoint *chorêgi*.

CA 300 *IG* II.² 3090

Inscription from Eleusis, end of 5th. century.

Gnathis son of Timocedes and Anaxandridas son of Timagoras were victorious *chorêgi* in the comedy competition with a play of Aristophanes; and won another victory in the tragedy competition with a play of Sophocles.

Lenaea:

CA 301 ARISTOPHANES, *Acharnians* 504–506, with Scholiast (cf. AE 83)

DIKAEOPOLIS. This is the festival of the Lenaea, and here we are with no strangers present yet: no tribute, no allies have come from the other states.

Scholiast: Drama was performed at the Lenaea while it was still winter, and it was ordained that states should bring their tribute to Athens for the Dionysia, as Eupolis says in his *Cities*.

CA 302 Scholiast on ARISTOPHANES, *Knights* 547

The Lenaea is an Athenian Festival in which, even to the present day, poets compete in writing compositions for comic effect. Demosthenes said that it derived from a wagon: singers used to recite and sing the compositions, seated on wagons.

CA 303 DEMOSTHENES 21.10

(Preamble to the Law of Evagoras)

During the days of the procession for Dionysus in Piraeus and the comedies and tragedies, and of the procession at the Lenaeum and the comedies and tragedies, and of the procession at the City Dionysia and the boys' performance and the merry-making (*kômos*) and the comedies and the tragedies, and of the procession and contest of Thargêlia, no one shall distrain on or appropriate another's goods, even for an overdue debt.

(For distraint, see CA 181)

The City Dionysia:

CA 304 ARISTOTLE, *Constitution of Athens* 56.2–5

2 The archon immediately on taking office first of all announces that whatever a man held before this time he shall keep and hold until the end
3 of the term of office. Next he appoints as *chorêgi* for the tragedies the three richest Athenians; previously he also appointed five *chorêgi* for the comedies, but nowadays the tribes nominate them. Next he summons also the *chorêgi* nominated by the tribes for the Dionysia to train the men and the boys and the comic choruses and for the Thargêlia to train the men and the boys (for the Dionysia one for two tribes, each tribe supplying one alternately) and settles with them all offers to exchange property and hears claims to have performed the service previously or to be exempt, on the grounds of a previous public service conferring an exemption which has not yet run out, or not to have reached the required age (*chorêgi* for the boys must be over 40).

He also appoints *chorêgi* for Delos and a chief of mission for the thirty-
4 oared ship which takes the unmarried youths. And he supervises processions, both that in honour of Asclepius when the initiates keep watch and that of the Great Dionysia, where he is helped by the Superintendents: previously these, ten in number, were chosen by the people on a show of hands and the people paid the expenses of the procession, but now he appoints one man from each tribe and gives him 100 minas for the
5 necessary gear. He also supervises the procession for the Thargêlia and for Zeus the Saviour. He also organises the competition at the Dionysia and the Thargêlia.

(*A man called upon to perform a liturgy could challenge anyone whom he thought wealthier to exchange properties or undertake the liturgy in his place*)

CA 305 ISOCRATES 8.82

Our forebears ... voted to split the surplus revenue into talents and bring it into the *orchêstra* at the Dionysia when the theatre was full: at the same time they brought into the theatre the children of those who had died in the war. This had the dual purpose of displaying to the allies the value of their capital brought in by hirelings and to the rest of Greece the number of orphans and the misfortunes brought about by this acquisitiveness.

(*Hirelings: probably a reference to the foreigners who helped to man the triremes which enforced collection of the tribute*)

CA 306 Scholiast on DEMOSTHENES 22.68

Among the Athenians it was the custom at the Dionysia and the Panathenaea to release prisoners from custody on bail for the occasion.

(*Demosthenes says that Androtion's father took advantage of this custom to escape*)

CA 307 HESYCHIUS, under *Allocation of Actors*

The poets were given three actors, assigned to them by lot, to perform their plays; the actor who won first prize qualified automatically for next year's competition.

CA 308 Scholiast on AESCHINES 3.67

A few days before the Great Dionysia in the building called the Odeum ... there was a display of the tragedies due to be performed in the theatre ... The actors came on without their masks on.

Chorus-training for the Dithyrambs:

CA 309 Scholiast on AESCHINES 1.11

The Athenians instituted choruses of fifty men or boys per tribe, so that there were ten choruses, the same number as the tribes.

CA 310 DEMOSTHENES 21.16–17

(*Demosthenes lodged a complaint against Midias for trying to sabotage his chorus*)

16   He actually planned to destroy the sacred vestments (for I regard as sacred all festival gear until it has been used) and the gold crowns which I had had made to adorn the chorus, by breaking into the goldsmith's house at

17   night. ... And not satisfied with that, he even bribed my chorus-trainer; and unless Telephanes, the oboe-player, had spotted the intrigue – bless him! – and got rid of my trainer and himself taken the responsibility of knocking the chorus into shape, we would not even have been in competition. The chorus would have entered untrained and we should have been disgraced. And that was not the limit of his monstrous behaviour. He had the effrontery to try to bribe the garlanded archon and organise the other *chorêgi* against me, shouting, threatening, standing by the judges as they took their oath, blocking the side-entrances and nailing them up, public property though they are.

CA 311 XENOPHON, *Memorabilia* 3.4.3–4

(*Nicomachides, whose name suggests "conquering in the fight", is disappointed because in spite of his fine military record he has not been elected general; instead the Athenians have chosen Antisthenes, a wealthy merchant*)

3   "You must remember" said Socrates, "that Antisthenes is also fond of winning, and that is an important quality in a general. Whenever he has acted as *chorêgus*, his chorus has always won, you recall."

"Maybe, but there is nothing in common between running a chorus and an army."

4   "But still, however little Antisthenes may have known about singing or chorus-training, he was nevertheless capable of finding the best people to do it for him."

Adjudication:

CA 312 PLUTARCH, *Cimon* 8.7

People also place to Cimon's credit the judgement in the tragedy-competition which became famous. For when Sophocles, who was as yet a young man, entered his first tragic chorus in competition, there was keen rivalry and partisanship among the spectators. So Apsephion the archon did not select the judges for the contest by lot, but, when Cimon came forward into the theatre with his fellow-generals and made the customary libations to the god, Apsephion did not allow them to depart, but bound them by oath and forced them to take the judges' seats, seeing that there were ten of them, one from each tribe.

Of the ten judges, only five were called upon, by lot, to declare their votes:

CA 313 LYSIAS 4.1, 3

1   It is strange, Councillors, for him to insist on claiming that we had not settled our differences and, while he couldn't deny that he had handed over the yoke of oxen and the slaves and the other things he had taken from his country-place under the exchange of properties, for him to deny, when all was clearly settled between us, that in the matter of this slave-girl, we had agreed to share the use of her . . .

3   I wish he had not failed in the lottery for judges at the Dionysia. He would then have shown you that we had come to terms by adjudging my tribe the winner; as it is, that was the verdict he wrote down on his tablet, but he was not one of the judges chosen.
      (*The identity of the people contesting this action is unknown*)

CA 314 PLATO, *Laws* 659a–c

The true judge must not take his cue from the theatre when giving his verdict or be dazed by the applause of the masses and his own philistine instincts, nor must he through feebleness or cowardice utter from the same

b   mouth which swore by the gods before his verdict an actual verdict which is untrue and irresponsible. The judge is properly not a pupil of the spectators but a teacher, and is there to resist those who try to give pleasure to them by unsuitable and wrong means. This was possible under the old Greek law, but not under the present Sicilian and Italian law, which allows a majority verdict of the spectators on a show of hands,

c   thereby corrupting the poets themselves, who descend to the low pleasure-standards of their judges and are educated by the spectators, and corrupting also the pleasures of the theatre; for whereas by always hearing plays above their own standards the spectators should have acquired a better kind of pleasure, in practice quite the opposite has happened.

The audience:

CA 315 PLATO, *Symposium* 175e

SOCRATES (*Alluding to Agathon's success with his tragedy*) . . . your talent manifested the day before yesterday before an audience of more than 30,000 fellow-Greeks.

CA 316 ATHENAEUS 11.464f

This is what Philochorus (*late-4th.-century Atthidographer*) says: "At the Dionysiac competitions the Athenians came to the theatre after first breakfasting and having a drink, and watched with garlands on their heads. Throughout the competition they poured out wine for themselves and provided themselves with confectionery . . . Evidence of this is also provided by Pherecrates the comic poet, saying that in his time the spectators were not without food."

(*The fruit eaten by the audience in the theatre could also be used as ammunition for pelting bad actors (Demosthenes 18.262)*)

CA 317 ANDOCIDES 4.20–21

20 Consider the case of Taureas who was rival *chorêgus* to Alcibiades in the boys' competition. The law decrees that anyone who wishes can eject without let or hindrance any foreigner competing in a chorus. But Alcibiades, before your own eyes and the eyes of the other Greek spectators and of all the archons in the city, drubbed Taureas out with blows; but since the spectators sided with Taureas, cheering his chorus

21 and refusing to listen to Alcibiades', the gesture was a flop. All the same, the judges, either in fright or in a desire to curry favour, gave him the victory, rating him of more importance than their oath.

CA 318 PLUTARCH, *Nicias* 29.2–3

(*The fate of the Athenians captured at Syracuse in 413 is being described*)

2 Some of them owed their release to Euripides. For it seemed that the Syracusans loved his work most of all the Greeks outside Athens. Whenever visitors arrived bringing show-passages and quotations with them, they would eagerly learn them and exchange them with each other.

3 At any rate on this occasion when the survivors returned home, many of them gave Euripides a warm greeting and explained that some of them had had their lives spared in captivity for teaching as many of his verses as they remembered; others had been given food and drink when they were wandering about after the battle, in return for singing his choral odes.

(b) THE SOCIAL FUNCTION OF COMEDY (CA 319–338)

The drama festivals brought together more Athenians into the same place at the same time than any other occasion. There was therefore no better opportunity for publicising ideas and advice. The dramatic poets were aware of this, and came to regard themselves as having a positive duty to deliver criticism, exhortation, and moral uplift. Aeschylus did not think it amiss to insert into the

Eumenides (e.g. 287–91, 667–73) propaganda for an alliance with Argos; and many passages in Euripides are evident testimonies to his admiration for democratic institutions (e.g. *Suppliants* 399–441, LACTOR 5 p.2) and his hatred of Sparta (e.g. *Andromache* 445–53). The tendency is much more marked in comedy, where the Parabasis provided an excuse for breaking the dramatic illusion and speaking directly to the audience about matters of moment; nowhere is there a clearer illustration than in Aristophanes, *Frogs* 686–737, LACTOR 5. p.55. Few contemporary politicians seem to have escaped the ridicule of the comic writers, although it is noticeable that the harshest criticism is reserved for demagogues and other extremists. Aristophanes was certainly not alone in looking back to the pre-Periclean era as the golden age of Athenian democracy; and others like him saw the potential danger of new educational ideas which undermined the traditional morality and left nothing in its place.

CA 319 ARISTOPHANES, *Frogs* 386–395

CHORUS OF INITIATES. Demeter, Lady of the sacred rites, stand by us, and preserve your chorus; grant that I may safely play and dance all day long; and that I may say many things in jest, many in earnest, and playing and joking in a manner worthy of your festival, I may win the victor's garland.
(*See also Frogs 686–7, LACTOR 5 p.55*)

CA 320 PLATONIUS, *Differences of Comedy* 1

Cratinus the poet of Old Comedy is harsh in his abuse, inasmuch as he imitates Archilochus. Unlike Aristophanes, who diffuses charm over his mockery, and so takes the coarseness out of his attacks, he goes bald-headed, as the saying is, into denouncing the offender.
(*Archilochus was an iambic poet of c.700–650 noted for his caustic style*)

CA 321 PLATONIUS, *Differences of Comedy* 1

Eupolis is incredibly imaginative in his plots; he gives his opening scenes plenty of impact, and evinces in the course of the drama itself imagination such as other poets show in the Parabasis: he is capable of bringing up the characters of lawgivers from Hades and through them proposing the passing or repeal of laws. His work is no less sublime and charming and his jokes are very well-aimed.

In spite of the violence of some of their attacks, the state only made a brief attempt to censor the works of comic writers.

CA 322 Scholiast on ARISTOPHANES, *Acharnians* 67

In the archonship of Euthymenes: this is the archon in whose time was rescinded the decree forbidding lampoon passed in the year of Morychides (*440*); it was valid for that year and the two that followed (the years of

Glaucinus and Theodorus), after which it was rescinded in the year of Euthymenes (*437*).

Views on politics:

CA 323 ARISTOPHANES, *Clouds* 549–559

CHORUS (*Parabasis*). I hit Cleon in the belly when he was at the height of
550   his power, but hadn't the heart to jump on him when he was down. But
       when the others have once got hold of Hyperbolus, they never leave off
553   pounding the poor man and his mother (*cf. CA 120*). First of all
       Eupolis dragged his *Maricas* on stage, turning our *Knights* inside out,
       the wretch, and making a mess of it, adding a drunken old woman just
       for the sake of the kordax (*an obscene dance*) – just as Phrynichus had
557   once done, when he had the sea-monster trying to eat her. Then
       Hermippus again laid into Hyperbolus, and now everyone else is
       muscling into Hyperbolus.
(*On Hyperbolus see also CA 54, 120*)

CA 324 ARISTOPHANES, *Acharnians* 676–701

676 CHORUS. We the old, the ancient, criticise the state; in our old age we
       are not looked after by you in a manner worthy of the sea-battles we
       fought, but we suffer dreadfully; you allow us old folks to be taken to
       court and laughed at by smart young orators, us mere nonentities,
683   tongue-tied and played out, with our sticks as our trusty Poseidon. And
       we take our stand in the court mumbling with age, seeing the case only
685   as fog. And the young man, all eager to plead his case, strikes quickly,
       tying him up with epigrams; then takes him by the scruff, and asks him
       questions full of traps and pitfalls, confusing and bemusing old
689   Tithonus and tearing him to shreds. And he can only mutter; then goes
692   off convicted; and with sobs and tears says to his friends: "Here am I
       fined all the money I had meant to pay for my coffin." How can it be
       right to destroy an old grey-beard over the water-clock, a man who
       bore his share of toil, and wiped the hot manly sweat in plenty off his
697   brow, a good man and true on the state's behalf at Marathon? We
       routed the foe at Marathon; now we are routed by worthless fellows,
       and brought to trial as well.
(*The water-clock was used for timing speeches in court – see p. 69*)

CA 325 ARISTOPHANES, *Knights* 1324–1334, 1365–1373

(*The Sausage-Seller brings in the news that Demos has been boiled down and rejuvenated*)

CHORUS. Can we see him? What's he wearing? What does he look like?
1325 SAUSAGE-SELLER. Like he was before when he was quartered with Aristides
      and Miltiades. But you'll see for yourself; you can hear the noise of the
      Propylaea gates opening. Raise a shout for the vision of ancient
      Athens, object of wonder and song, where famous Demos dwells.
1329 CHORUS. O shining Athens, violet-crowned, the envy of all, reveal to us the
      Lord of Greece and of this land.

SAUSAGE-SELLER. See him come, with his grasshopper hair-clip, gleaming in the garments of old, redolent not of jury-votes, but of peace-treaties, and anointed with myrrh.

CHORUS. Hail, King of the Greeks; we rejoice with you, for your deeds are worthy of the city and of the Marathon trophy.

(*Demos repents of his former corruptible ways*)

1365 SAUSAGE-SELLER. Tell me, what will your policy be in general?

DEMOS. First of all, when the rowers bring the warships to land, I will pay them their wages in full.

SAUSAGE-SELLER. That will be a favour to all those buttocks worn flat on the rowing-benches.

1369 DEMOS. Then if a hoplite is given a posting, he can try as hard as he likes to find a substitute, but he'll have to stick to his original posting in the end.

SAUSAGE-SELLER. That's taken a bite out of Cleonymus' shield-strap.

DEMOS. And no smooth-faced boys will loiter in the agora.

(*Cleonymus was ridiculed for throwing away his shield in battle*)

CA 326 EUPOLIS, *Demes* fr. 117

I don't know what I can say with all these people here, I'm so distressed by the present state of the city. This isn't how we old folk used to live once, but first of all we had in the city generals from the greatest families, pre-eminent in wealth and breeding, whom we prayed to as gods. So we were quite secure; but now we go campaigning any old where, with mere riff-raff as our elected generals.

CA 327 EUPOLIS, *Cities* fr. 205

We have now got as generals men whom in the past we wouldn't even have chosen to provide the festival lamps. O city, city! You may be fortunate, but you've got no sense.

CA 328 PLATO (*Comicus*) fr. 186

If one wicked man dies, two politicians spring up. For we have no Heracles in the city to burn off the heads of the politicians. You have prostituted yourself; so you'll be a politician.

CA 329 PLUTARCH, *Pericles* 3.2–3

2 When he was born, Pericles' physical form was perfect except that his head was elongated out of proportion. For this reason statues almost always show him wearing a helmet, presumably because the craftsmen did not wish to discredit him. But the Attic comic poets called him "Squill-head"

3 ... Like Cratinus in *The Chirons* who says: "Strife and ancestral Cronus mated and produced the biggest tyrant of all, whom the gods call 'head-gatherer'".

(Head-gatherer: a pun on the Homeric epithet for Zeus – "cloud-gatherer")

CA 330 PLUTARCH, *Pericles* 13.5–6

5   The Odeum, whose internal arrangements included many seats and pillars, and whose circular roof was made in the form of a cone, was said to have been copied from the Persian King's pavilion. The work was

6   among those instigated by Pericles. This was why Cratinus again made fun of him in his *Thracian Women*: "Here comes squill-headed Zeus, with the Odeum on his head now that the Ostrakon has passed".

(The Ostrakon is a reference to attempts to have Pericles banished ("ostracised"). On Pericles, see also Eupolis fr. 94, LACTOR 5 p. 13)

CA 331 EUPOLIS fr. 158

B. Let Alcibiades leave the ranks of the women.

ALCIBIADES. What's this nonsense? Go home and keep your wife in training.

CA 332 PLATO (*Comicus*) fr. 187

(On Hyperbolus) (see CA 54)

And yet this (ostracism) was right for men of earlier days, quite wrong for him, the "branded slave". It was not for such as him that ostracism was invented.

CA 333 EUPOLIS fr. 31

Pisander went on campaign against Spartolus and there he was the biggest coward in the whole army.

(Pisander was a leader of the extreme oligarchs in 412–411)

Views on education:

CA 334 EUPOLIS fr. 146

Inside is Protagoras of Teos, who, evil imposter that he is, tells lies about heavenly matters and eats the fruits of the earth.

(On Protagoras, see Index)

CA 335 CRATINUS fr. 155

There live people who describe the sky and convince us it's an oven and that it's all round us and we are the charcoal.

This idea was said to have come from Hippon of Samos. Aristophanes also makes fun of it in *Clouds* 95–97 (CA 218).

CA 336 ARISTOPHANES, *Broilermen* (fr. 490)

This man has been ruined either by a book or by Prodicus, or one of those idle babblers.

(*On Prodicus, see also CA 214–5, 294, 395 ff.*)

CA 337 ARISTOPHANES, *Birds* 992–1011

(*The foundation of Cloudcuckooland is interrupted by the arrival of another bureaucrat*)

METON. I am here –
PISTHETAERUS. Here's another nuisance. What do you want? What sort of thing have you in mind? What is your intent? What boots your journey?
995 METON. I want to measure the air, and divide it into acres for you.
PISTHETAERUS. Who are you for heaven's sake?
METON. Me! I'm Meton, well known to Greece and Colonus.
PISTHETAERUS. Tell me, what's that you've got?
1000 METON. It's an air-ruler. You see, the air as a whole is shaped like a bread-oven (*cf. CA 335*). So if I lay the ruler here, and then above it I put the point of the dividers you see?
PISTHETAERUS. No I don't.
1004 METON. I put the ruler down and measure it out in a straight line, and there you have a nicely squared circle, with an agora in the middle, and straight roads converging there, like rays shining out in all directions from a circular star.
1010 PISTHETAERUS. The man's a Thales. Meton?
METON. What?
PISTHETAERUS. My dear, dear fellow – just do as I say and clear off.

CA 338 EUPOLIS fr. 352

I also hate the talkative beggar Socrates, who has got plenty of ideas in his head, but hasn't bothered to think where his next meal is to come from.

(c) MUSIC (CA 339–348)

The fifth and fourth centuries BC saw changes both in the style and in the social status of music. The upper classes of Aristotle's generation had a conspicuously lower regard for it than, say, that of Aristophanes. Attitudes held up to scorn by Aristophanes are taken for granted by Aristotle. There was also a stylistic revolution, accompanied by vigorous critical controversy (to which we owe a good deal of our information). The older fashion embraced a number of sharply distinct traditional styles. From the mid-fifth century on a new school grew up, who for expressive effect combined and switched between the styles, besides more technical innovations such as modulation of mode and key, directly imitative effects, and increased virtuosity in performance. Apart from those mentioned in these passages, an important figure was Euripides (cf. Aristophanes, *Frogs, passim*). The two fashions coexisted well into the fourth century.

The following explanatory notes may also be helpful for this section:

Musical terms:
  harmoniai: lyre-tunings for particular styles, so perhaps 'Modes'

paean: song of thanksgiving to Apollo, especially of triumph or defiance in
    battle
dithyramb: narrative choral song in honour of Dionysus
nomes: a group of musical forms, some of great antiquity, consisting
    probably of melodic formulae to which narrative words could be set

Instruments:
    pipes (auloi):   always in pairs, with cylindrical bore sounded by double
        reeds; *not* flutes.
    lyre: normally with seven strings, increased to 11 or 12 by 'modernists';
        tortoise-shell sound-box
    cithara: elaborate concert variety of lyre with enlarged sound-box
    barbitos: lyre with 10 strings, associated with Alcaeus, Sappho, Anacreon
    pêctis, sambuca: types of harp, as were (probably) the heptagon and trigon

Musicians:
    Aristoxenus of Tarentum, c.375–320. Pupil of Aristotle and musicologist.
    Melanippides of Melos, fl. c.450–425. Ranked as one of the greatest
        musicians (Xen.*Mem*.1.4.3)
    Philoxenus, c.435–380. Reputedly once slave and apprentice to
        Melanippides.
    Timotheus, 447–357. One of the leading innovators.

The place of music in society:

CA 339 EURIPIDES, *Heracles* 673–686

> CHORUS OF THEBAN ELDERS. I shall never leave off mingling the Graces
> with the Muses, sweetest of unions. May I never live without music, but
> always live among the poets' garlands. Even an aged singer still sounds
> the strain of Memory. Still I sing the victory-song of Heracles, to the
> accompaniment of Bromius the wine-giver, or to the tune of the seven-
> stringed lyre and the Libyan pipe. Not yet shall I lay aside the Muses
> who set me dancing.

CA 340 ARISTOTLE, *Politics* 1337b–1342b (extracts)

1337b   As to the study of music there might be dispute. Most people nowadays
    take part in it for pleasure; but others originally established it in education
    because human nature itself seeks, as I have often said, not merely to work
    rightly but to be able to use our leisure well.
1338a   Our predecessors, then, established music in education not as essential
    (there is nothing of that about it), nor as of practical utility... There
    remains utility for the conduct of our leisure, apparently the grounds on
    which men do introduce it. For therein they prescribe what they consider
    conduct of leisure fit for a free man.
        ...(The purpose of music is not mere amusement even in childhood.
    And whatever its purpose, is there any reason for making people practise

it themselves rather than just listening to professionals? Before deciding that, we should consider its educational value.) . . .

. . . Melodies on the other hand (*as opposed to pictorial likenesses*) in themselves represent states of character. This is obvious. To start with, the natures of the *harmoniai* are distinct, so that the hearers are differently

1340b   affected and react in a different fashion to each of them. To some mournfully and dispiritedly as to the one called 'in the Mixolydian manner'; to some with a relaxed mentality, as to the 'slack' (? low-pitched) ones; in a moderate and steadfast way to one other in particular – the *harmonia* 'in the Dorian manner' seems to have this effect uniquely; rapturously to the one 'in the Phrygian manner'. This is said by those who have made a philosophical study of this aspect of education; rightly, for their theories are derived from actual facts. The same sort of thing goes for rhythms . . .

We must now consider, as I said before, whether or not they should study by singing and physically playing themselves. Clearly enough, it makes a great difference to what sort of person you become if you practise music-making yourself. It is difficult or impossible for those who do not practise doing it to become proper and serious judges. Clearly then, music should be taught in a way that involves the practice of music-making.

1341a   . . . The proper consequences would follow in education if no pains were taken over what leads to contests of professional skill, nor to the excessive and spectacular feats that have now come into competitions and from them into education; rather *this* sort of music (and just to the point when they can appreciate fine melodies and rhythms, not merely the common sort of music that can be appreciated by some kinds of animals, let alone by the mob of slaves and children).

From this it is also clear which instruments should be used. The pipes should not be taken for education, nor any other instrument requiring technical accomplishment, such as the cithara or anything else like it, but instruments that will improve their hearers in their musical or other education. Besides, the pipe is not an instrument expressive of moral character, but rather an orgiastic one, so it should be used on those occasions when the object in view is the regulation of emotions (catharsis) rather than instruction. We may add that it has consequences the reverse of educational in that piping oneself prevents the use of words. Consequently our predecessors were right to reject its use by children and free men, though earlier still they did use it. For with the growth of wealth and leisure, and more self-confident notions of excellence, after the Persian wars and just before, they were encouraged by their achievements to grasp at all kinds of study, seeking out new ones without discrimination. And so the study of the pipes was introduced into education. Even in Sparta there was a *chorêgus* who piped for the chorus himself, while in Athens it became so fashionable that perhaps the majority of free men took it up. . . . Later, out of experience, it was rejected, as men became better able to decide what contributes to worth and what does not; as were many other old-fashioned instruments such as the pêctis and barbitos, and those

1341b   that titillate the ear of the audience – the heptagon, trigon and sambuca, and all that require manual skill. There is also a point in the story told by the ancients about the pipes. They say in fact that Athena invented them and threw them away. It is fair enough to say that the goddess did so in disgust at her ugly expression. All the same, it is more reasonable that it was because education in piping does nothing for the intelligence. We must attribute to Athena understanding as well as skill.

1342a   But for education (*as opposed to public performance*) as I said, those melodies expressive of moral character should be used, and the *harmoniai* of the same sort: the one 'in the Dorian manner' for instance as mentioned earlier. We must also accept any others recommended by those with experience of both philosophical enquiry and musical education. The Socrates of the *Republic* is wrong to leave only the one 'in the Phrygian manner' besides the Dorian, especially as he rejects the pipes among

1342b   instruments. Among *harmoniai* the one 'in the Phrygian manner' has the same force as the pipes do among instruments; both are emotional and orgiastic. Poetry shows this. For every Bacchic frenzy and every agitation of the kind belong particularly to the pipes, while of the *harmoniai* they find fit expression in melodies 'in the Phrygian manner'. The dithyramb for instance seems by common consent to be a Phrygian melody. Those concerned with understanding the matter give many examples of this, in particular that Philoxenus attempted to compose his dithyramb *The Mysians* 'in the Dorian manner' and could not, but was forced by the very nature of the case to revert to the suitable *harmonia*, that 'in the Phrygian manner'.

CA 341 PLUTARCH, *Alcibiades* 2.4–6

4   When Alcibiades went to school, he paid proper attention to the rest of his teachers, but refused to play the pipes on the grounds that it was unfitting for a free man and a gentleman: he claimed that the use of the lyre and plectrum did nothing to disfigure the looks and bearing proper to a gentleman; but when a man blew the pipes, even his family had difficulty recognising him. Moreover the lyre blended and harmonised with the voice of the player, whereas the pipe blocked the mouth and took away the power of singing and speaking . . . (*Alcibiades therefore gave up the*

6   *pipes and persuaded others to do the same*) . . . As a result pipe-playing came to be dropped from the liberal curriculum and utterly despised.

CA 342 PLATO, *Laws* 812d–e

For these purposes (in education) they need to make use of the notes of the lyre, because of the distinct sound of the strings, and the music teacher and his pupil should produce note in unison with note; as for differing notes and ornamentation on the lyre, with the strings sounding a tune different from that of the poet who composed the song, when they even produce a blend of narrow intervals against wide, swift notes against slow or high

e   against low, and likewise fit all sorts of elaborate rhythms to the notes of the lyre – well all that sort of thing should contribute nothing to children who are going to be taught all that is valuable in music swiftly in three years. Conflict and confusion in the subject make learning difficult, and the young must learn as easily as possible.

The musical revolution:

CA 343 PLATO, *Laws* 700a–701a

700a I mean in the first place the laws there were then about music, if we may trace the advance of excessive free living from its origin. For in those days
 b   we had our music divided by types, the forms it took, as it were; one type of song was prayers to the gods – they were known as hymns; there was another type of the very opposite of these, dirges would be the best term; paeans were another, yet another was called dithyramb... Nomes, as another kind of song were called by that very name; they were qualified as nomes sung to the lyre. These and some more were kept distinct, and it was not allowed to misuse one kind of melody by mixing it into another.
 c   The authority to recognise them and thereupon to judge – and for that matter to punish any who disobeyed – was not wolf-whistles, or any musicless shouts from the mob either, as nowadays, nor yet the clapping that renders applause. No, it was an established rule for those concerned with education to listen in silence themselves till the end of the piece, and as for the children and their attendants and the crowd in general, there was the discipline of the stick to keep them in order.
 d   Disciplined thus in music, the mass of citizens were willing to be ruled, and did not dare to judge by uproar. Later, as time went on, there came poets who began the unmusical lawlessness – naturally gifted poets, but ignorant of what was right and fair for Music. Intoxicated, controlled by pleasure rather than by what was needed, they mixed dirges with hymns, and paeans with dithyrambs, imitated pipe songs in their lyre songs –
 e   joined, in fact, everything with everything else. Thus, not deliberately, but out of folly, they spread the falsehood about music that there is no such thing as right and wrong in music, and that it is by the pleasure of the man who enjoys it, be he a good man or a bad, that one judges what is most correct. By creating works like that, and adding doctrines like that, they inculcated in the majority a lawlessness about music and an arrogant claim to be competent judges. Consequently audiences once mute became
701a vociferous, as if they were discerning musical critics of good and bad – in place of aristocracy in music came a vicious theatocracy. Now if a sort of democracy of free men had happened in this alone, nothing very terrible would have happened, but in fact from our music began the lawless fancy of universal wisdom about everything, and free politics followed.

CA 344 PHERECRATES, *Chiron* fr. 145

(*Enter Music, a young woman visibly molested. Justice asks what has happened to her*)

MUSIC. I will be glad to tell you; you may enjoy hearing the tale as I will reciting it. My woes began with Melanippides, the first of them to take
 5   and undo me, make me a loose woman (*lit. more unstrung*) with his dozen strings; but all the same he could be borne compared with what I

10

15

20

25

suffer now . . . Cinesias (*fl.420*), that cursed Athenian, makes loops (=
modulations) out of key in his stanzaic songs, and reduces me to such a
state that when he writes his dithyrambs it's like reflections in a shield
(?), the right seems left behind! But I could bear him all the same. Now
Phrynis (*fl.c.445*) threw in some twiddle of his own, looped me and
twisted and utterly destroyed me; his pentachords gave a dozen modes
at once. Still even him I could put up with – if he did any wrong he put
it right again. But Timotheus, Oh Darling!, he's quite buried me, and
ground me up outrageously.

JUSTICE. Who is this man Timotheus?

MUSIC. Redhead from Miletus. The wrong he's done me quite outstrips the
rest I mentioned, with the ant-run twists he'd led me up. And if ever he
met me on a walk alone, he made free verse and free love, with twelve
strings.

(*pentachord: instead of the tetrachord (four notes within a perfect fourth),
which was the normal building block of the Greek scale*)

  (*The passage is full of sexual double-entendre; for instance the word for
'string' is also a colloquialism for 'penis'*)

CA 345 PLUTARCH, *Moralia* 1142b–c (*On Music*)

Aristoxenus says that one of his contemporaries, Telesias the Theban,
chanced to be brought up on the finest music, and be taught the works of
such highly reputed men as Pindar, Dionysius the Theban, Lamprus,
Pratinas, and all the other lyric poets who were good composers of string

c   music. He was also a fine pipe player, and thoroughly well trained in all
other aspects of the subject. In middle age, however he was so powerfully
seduced by the elaborate music of the stage that he despised the noble
works on which he was brought up, and learned inside out the works of
Philoxenus and Timotheus, and even of those the ones most elaborate and
containing most innovation. When he made a start at composing music,
he attempted both styles, Pindar's and Philoxenus', but was unable to
succeed with Philoxenus' kind of music. And the reason was his excellent
upbringing from childhood.

  (*Dionysius was teacher to the great general Epaminondas, and Lamprus
(reputedly) to Sophocles*)

Aristophanes makes frequent uncomplimentary references to the new music
(e.g. *Clouds* 969–70), and parodies its style, notably in *Frogs* 1309–63, and in the
passage preceding this excerpt.

CA 346 ARISTOPHANES, *Thesmophoriazusae* 64–69

(*A servant has just announced, in the most extravagantly lyrical terms, that
his master Agathon is about to begin composing*)

EURIPIDES. You there, please call Agathon out to me here, by hook or by
crook.

SERVANT. No need even to ask. He'll be out himself directly. You see, he's beginning to compose the music. This winter weather it's hard to loop his stanzas round, unless he brings them out and lays them in the sun.

CA 347 TIMOTHEUS, *Persae* fr. 12.203–234

(From the concluding section of what is said to be a nome)

Now, O exalter of a new-wrought Muse with golden lyre, come to aid my songs, hail Paean. For the long lived, great ruler of noble Sparta, and the people swelling with the flower of youth, terrify me, and, kindling with a blaze of censure, drive me away, because I dishonour an older Muse with new songs. But I keep no man out of these songs, new, old, or my own age; only the archaic corrupters of music, those I do keep away, the outragers of song, who stretch out the yells of the town crier with his shrill far-carrying voice.

Orpheus was the first father of elaborate music on the lyre, son of Calliope . . . from Pieria. Terpander in his songs yoked the Muse to the ten (*? tunes*). Aeolian Lesbos bore him to be the glory of Antissa. Now Timotheus brings a lyre to birth in measures and rhythms of eleven notes, opening a treasure of many songs for a cloistered muse.

CA 348 PRATINAS fr. 1

(This excerpt comes probably from a satyr play; the chorus are complaining at the way the accompanying pipe-music has begun to take precedence over the words of the dithyramb)

What is this utter hubbub, what is this dancing around? What insult has come on the sore-trampled altar of Dionysus? Bromius is mine, mine, so I should shout and stamp, running over the mountains with the Naeads, and singing a melody like the intricate-winged swan. Song is the queen the Muse has made – the pipe must follow after – yes, he is a servant; he only wants to be leader of revels, general of gate-crashing, brawling young drunks. Beat the man with the mottled breath of a toad! Burn the spittle-spoiling reed, the chatter bawler, the strutting time-and-tune-spoiler, body faked up with a drill! Look at me. This is the shaking of hand and foot; Lord Thriambus of the dithyramb with the ivy in your hair, look, look at my Dorian dance.

(Bromius and Thriambus are both names of Dionysus (cf. CA 339))

(d) THE VISUAL ARTS

The excerpts in this section, containing description of both extant and lost works, and some discussion of aesthetics, are of course only intended to complement the study of Athenian art through a well illustrated text-book; the important topic of vase painting is omitted altogether because of the absence of literary evidence.

1. Architecture and Sculpture (CA 349–368)

During the Periclean period Athens was fortunate in having the opportunity, the funds and the expertise to create the finest public buildings in the Greek world. For religious reasons the Acropolis temples destroyed by the Persians in 480 had not yet been rebuilt; the annual tribute of the Empire had accumulated a surplus of thousands of talents; and the development of the Doric style of architecture had just reached new heights of grandeur and sophistication in the Temple of Zeus at Olympia. Pericles was anxious to make a showpiece out of Athens, and he required the backing of state-funds; in spite of some opposition to his appropriation of imperial revenues, and the intervention of the Peloponnesian War, an astonishing programme of building was carried out.

The buildings also offered unprecedented scope for artists, since sculpture and painting were integral parts of architectural design. The giant gold-and-ivory statues of Phidias commanded more world-wide admiration than any other single product of the Periclean age. They have long perished, but the descriptions that survive give an idea of the impression they created.

CA 349 DEMOSTHENES 3.25–26

25   How our ancestors regarded the city itself is evident both in their public
and their private buildings. At public expense they created buildings and
adornments for them, in the way of temples and the votive offerings
within, of a quality and number unsurpassable by any subsequent
generation: meanwhile as individuals they were so modest and so careful

26   to observe the democratic spirit that, if anyone knows what the house is
like in which Aristides or Miltiades or one of the heroes of those days
lived, he can see that it is no more imposing than the house next door: for
they did not conduct the affairs of the city with a view to acquiring private
capital, but every man thought it his duty to improve the common weal.

Domestic architecture:

CA 350 XENOPHON, *Memorabilia* 3.8.8–10

8   Socrates in my opinion stated an important principle of architecture,
9   when he said that a practical house was also a beautiful one . . . "In houses
facing south, the sun in winter shines right into the porch, but in summer
we are shaded from it as it goes over our heads and over the rooftops.
Now if this arrangement is a good one, we ought to build the south-facing
parts higher, to make the most of the winter sun, and the north-facing

10   parts lower, to avoid the blasts of the north wind. Putting it in a nutshell, a
house where a man can find the most agreeable shelter for himself and the
safest repository for his possessions all the year round may reasonably be
regarded as the most agreeable and the most beautiful dwelling-place.
Paintings and decorations detract from the cheerfulness of the place more
than they contribute to it."

CA 351 XENOPHON, *Memorabilia* 3.1.7

(*Socrates to Dionysodorus*)

"There is a great difference between an army that is well deployed and one
that is not; just as stones, bricks, timbers and tiles thrown together
haphazardly are useless, but when the materials that do not rot or wear
away, the stones and tiles, are placed underneath and over the top, and the

bricks and timbers are put in the middle – as one does when building – then the result is a valuable possession, a house."

Private dedications:

CA 352 PLUTARCH, *Cimon* 13.6,8

The aftermath of Cimon's successful campaign against the Persians on the Eurymedon, c. 467.

6   When the spoils of war had been sold, the people were able to finance a number of projects, including the construction of the southern wall of the Acropolis, which was paid for out of the proceeds of that campaign ... (Cimon personally contributed to the building of the foundations of the

8   Long Walls) ... Cimon was the first to adorn the city with the so-called genteel and elegant leisure-centres which became exceedingly popular a little later: he planted the agora with plane-trees and transformed the grove of the Academy from its barren and waterless state into a place flowing with streams and furnished with properly designed running-tracks and thickly shaded walks.

CA 353 ML 44

Decree connected with the building of the temple of Athena Nike,? 450–445

5   ... To make a door for the shrine in accordance with Callicrates' designs ...

11   ... to build a temple in accordance with Callicrates' designs, and a stone altar.

    (For the chronological problems, see ML pp. 109–111) (Callicrates was one of the architects of the Parthenon, with Ictinus, CA 356)

The Periclean programme:

CA 354 PLUTARCH, *Pericles* 12.5–7

5   Pericles put before the people great plans for building projects, and suggestions for operations involving many crafts over a considerable time, so that the home-based section of the population might with justification profit from a share in the state's wealth, no less than the soldiers and

6   sailors on guard or on campaign. The materials were to be stone, bronze, ivory, gold, ebony, and cypress-wood; and the crafts required to work these up were those of the carpenter, the moulder, the metalworker, the mason, the worker of gold and ivory, the painter, the pattern-maker, the engraver. Then there were all the people who transported and carried the

7   materials – the merchants and sailors and helmsmen on sea, and the wagon-makers and keepers of draught-animals on land together with the makers of rope and cloth, and the cobblers and road-builders and miners; and each craft had its own crowd of unskilled workers attached to it, like a general with a private army.

(*The reliability of this account is questioned by A. Andrewes in JHS 1978 p. 3*)

CA 355 PLUTARCH, *Pericles* 31.2–4

Attacks on the friends of Pericles:

2   But the worst charge of all, and the one for which there was the greatest number of witnesses is broadly as follows:

Phidias the sculptor contracted for the making of the statue, as has been said. He had become a friend of Pericles and had acquired great influence with him. But he had excited the enmity of some people because of their envy towards him, while others wanted to test the opinion of the people in his case, to see what kind of a judge it would be for Pericles; so they persuaded Menon, one of Phidias' assistants, to sit as a suppliant in the agora, begging for a pardon in return for laying information and bringing

3   a charge against Phidias. The people accepted his story, and an action was brought in the Assembly, but the acts of theft were not proved. For Phidias had worked the gold plate separately, at Pericles' suggestion, and had applied it to the statue from the outset in such a way that it was possible to remove it all and weigh it – as Pericles ordered the accusers to do there and then.

4   However the glory of his works of art was a burden to Phidias because of the jealousy they aroused, and above all because, when depicting the battle against the Amazons on the shield, he had carved a figure of himself as a bald-headed old man raising a rock in both hands, and incorporated into the design a very handsome likeness of Pericles fighting against an Amazon. Yet the position of the hand as it held up the spear in front of Pericles' face had been skilfully done so as to hide the likeness, which is however visible on either side of it.

CA 356 VITRUVIUS 7, *Preface* 16

(*Listed among marble temples of particular excellence*)

At Eleusis Ictinus built a temple to Ceres and Proserpine; it was in the Dorian style, of immense size, without exterior columns, and covered over to make an open space for sacrificing.

CA 357 *IG* I². 374, 56–74, 82–114, 161–183, 223–233

From the Erechtheum building accounts of 408–6

To those who put up the curved roof; fitting a cross-beam into its bed and

60   all the others into theirs; to Manis resident at Collytus 1dr.; to Croesus resident in the deme of the Scambonides 1dr.; to Andreas resident in Melite 1dr.; to Prepon resident in Agryle 1dr.; to Medus resident in Melite 1dr.; to Apollodorus resident in Melite 1dr.

To the six men who took down the scaffolding from the columns in the

70   porch: Teucrus resident in Cydathenaeus 1dr.; Cerdon slave of Axipeithes 1dr.; Croesus resident in the deme of the Scambonides 1dr.; Prepon resident in Agryle 1dr.; Cephisodorus 1dr.; Spodias 1dr. . . .

82   To the sawyers working by the day, two men working at a drachma a
        day each for sixteen days: to Rhaedius resident in Collytus and his mate,
90   32dr.; to sawyers working by the day in the third fortnight (*lit. twelve-day
        period*) on sheathing planks for the roof, two men working for a drachma
        a day each for seven days: to Rhaedius resident in Collytus and his mate,
        14dr. Total for the sawyers 46dr.
             To the encaustic painters: for painting the moulding on the interior
100   architrave at five obols a foot, the contractor Dionysodorus resident in
        Melite, the guarantor Heraclides from Oea, 30dr. Total for encaustic
        painters, 30dr.
             To the goldsmiths: to Sisyphus resident in Melite for gilding the rosettes
        we paid the sums owing during the previous prytany of the Oeneid tribe.
        Total for the goldsmiths (. . .)
110   Fees: to the architect Archilochus from Agryle 37dr., to the assistant
        secretary Pyrgion 30dr. 5ob. Total Fees: 67dr. 5ob. Total of all expenses:
        1790dr. $3\frac{1}{2}$ob.
161   Phyromachus of Cephisia: the young man beside the breastplate 60dr.;
        Praxias resident in Melite: the horse and the man visible behind it (*or, seen
        from behind*) pushing it sideways, 120dr.; Antiphanes from Cerameis: the
170   chariot and the young man and the pair of horses being yoked, 240dr.;
        Phyromachus of Cephisia: the man leading the horse, 50dr.; Mynnium
        resident in Agryle: the horse and man beating it, and the pillar that he
        added later, 127dr.; Soclus resident in Alopece: the man holding the
        bridle, 60dr.; Phyromachus of Cephisia: the man leaning on the stick
180   beside the altar, 60dr.; Iasus of Collytus: the woman being embraced by
        the girl, 80dr. Total for the sculpture: 3315dr. . . . .
223   For fluting the columns facing the altar on the same side as the altar of
        Dione: Laossus of Alopece 20dr., Philon of Erchia 20dr., Parmenon slave
230   of Laossus 20dr., Carion slave of Laossus 20dr.; next in order: Phalacrus
        of Paeania 20 dr., Philostratus of Paeania 20dr., Thargelion slave of
        Phalacrus 20dr., Philurgus (= *Work-lover*) slave of Phalacrus 20dr.,
        Gerys slave of Phalacrus 20dr.

A section from the accounts of the year 409–8 (*IG* I². 373) is translated on pp.
115–6 of C. Mossé: *The Ancient World at Work* (Chatto and Windus, Ancient
Culture and Society series, 1969).

The work of Phidias:

CA 358 PAUSANIAS 1.28.2

The Athenians have two dedications from the tithe of war-spoils; one is a
bronze statue of Athena (Promachos) derived from the Persian landing at
Marathon, the work of Phidias. They say that the engraving of the Battle
of Lapiths and Centaurs on the shield and the rest of the relief-work was
done by Mys to the designs of Parrhasius son of Evenor. The spear-point
and helmet-crest of this Athena can actually be seen by people sailing from
Sunium. . . . The most noteworthy of Phidias' works is the statue of
Lemnian Athena, so called after the people who dedicated it.

CA 359 NICETAS OF CHONAE, *History of the Emperor Isaac Angelus and his son Alexis,* **p. 738B** (see H. Stuart-Jones: *Ancient writers on Greek Sculpture* p. 78).

> (*Describing the sack of Constantinople in AD 1203–4, the writer gives many details of the statues then destroyed, including the Athena Promachos*)

It stood up straight to a height of thirty feet, and its clothing was of the same bronze material as the whole image. The robe reached down to the feet and was bunched up in several places ... A girdle of Ares held her quite tightly round the waist. On her chest with its prominent breasts she had a complicated overgarment like an aegis hanging down from the shoulders and representing the Gorgon's head. The long extent of her neck, left uncovered by the dress, was an irresistible sight ... Individual veins stood out, and the whole body was supple and properly articulated ... On her head was a horsehair crest which "nodded terribly from above" (*cf. Homer, Iliad 3.336–7*). Her hair was plaited and tied back, but you could feast your eyes on the locks which poured over her forehead and were not quite concealed by her helmet.

CA 360 PAUSANIAS 1.24.5, 7

5   As one enters the temple called the Parthenon everything on the pediment bears upon the birth of Athena; the other end is the quarrel of Poseidon with Athena over the country. The statue itself is made of ivory and gold. On the middle of the helmet is set a sphinx ... and griffins worked on each
7   side of it ... The statue of Athena is upright in an ankle-length tunic, and the head of Medusa is engraved in ivory on her breast, and she has a Victory about four cubits high, and a spear in her hand and a shield lying at her feet, and near the spear is a snake which might be Erichthonius. On the plinth of the statue is worked the birth of Pandora.

CA 361 PLINY, *Natural History* 36.18

> (*Pliny cites the shield of the Athena Parthenos as particular evidence of Phidias' genius*)

On the convex side he engraved the Battle of the Amazons, and on the concave, the fights between Gods and Giants; on the sandals there were the Lapiths and Centaurs fighting, which shows that even the smallest area had artistic potential for him. The subject engraved on the base is called "The Birth of Pandora", with twenty gods attending. The figure of Victory is particularly remarkable, but experts also admire the golden snake at the butt of the spear, and the Sphinx.

CA 362 QUINTILIAN, *Oratorical Education* 12.10.9

Phidias is reckoned to be an artist better at making statues of gods than of men; in fact he has no rival at all in gold-and-ivory – even if he had done nothing else except the Athena Parthenos and the Olympian Zeus at Elis, whose beauty seems even to add something to the god's acknowledged divinity; so well did the majesty of the work match the godhead.

CA 363 CICERO, *Orator* 8–9

(Cicero is discussing the nature of the Ideal, which one can only grasp with the mind, not the senses)

8
9   Though the statues of Phidias are, to our eyes, the most perfect of their kind, we can imagine ones more beautiful. When that artist was making his Zeus or Athena he surely did not have before his eyes an individual whose likeness he could copy, but in his own mind there was some outstanding image of beauty, which he would concentrate on and so direct his skill and his hand to representing it.

CA 364 JULIAN THE APOSTATE, *Letters* 377A, B

Much can be displayed in a little. The clever Phidias did not only get his reputation from the statues at Olympia and Athens, but he knew how to encompass a work of great art even in a tiny carving, like his grasshopper

B   and his bee apparently, or if you like, his fly; each of these things was given life by his art, though in fact made of bronze.

The followers of Phidias:

CA 365 PLINY, *Natural History* 36.15–17

15
16   Phidias himself is said to have sculpted in marble, and there is in Octavia's collection at Rome a Venus of his of exceptional beauty. There is no doubt also that he was the teacher of Alcamenes, a leading exponent, several of whose works are to be found in temples at Athens, and outside the city is a remarkable statue of Venus called "Aphrodite in the Gardens"; Phidias himself is said to have put the last touches to the work.

17   Another of his pupils was Agoracritus of Paros, who was such a favourite because of his youthful beauty, that Phidias allowed his own name to be given to some of his works. Both pupils competed in making an Aphrodite; Alcamenes won, not on merit, but because the Athenians supported one of their citizens against a foreigner. Whereupon Agoracritus sold his, on condition it should not remain at Athens, and called it Nemesis. This is now to be found in Rhamnous, an Attic deme.

CA 366 PLINY, *Natural History* 34.74

Cresilas made the following: a man dying from his wounds (you can see just how little life is left in him), a wounded Amazon, and a Pericles, worthy of his title, "The Olympian".

CA 367 PLINY, *Natural History* 34.81

Styppax of Cyprus is renowned for one statue, "The offal-roaster"; this represents a slave of Pericles grilling offal, and puffing up the fire with full cheeks.

CA 368 XENOPHON, *Memorabilia* 3.10.6–8

6   Once Socrates went to see the sculptor Cliton, and said to him in the course of conversation: "I can see for myself that the statues you make of

runners, wrestlers, boxers and pancratiasts are beautiful. But how do you
create in them the illusion of vitality which does most to attract the person

7   looking at them?" Cliton was unable to think of an answer at once, so he
continued: "Well, do you make your statues appear more lifelike by
copying the forms of living people?"

"Certainly" he said.

"So by copying the parts of the body in different attitudes, as they are
moved up and down, contracted and stretched, tensed and relaxed, you
represent them in a more realistic and convincing manner?"

"That's right."

8   "And does not the beholder also appreciate the representation of what
the person doing something feels?"

"I should have thought so."

"So you must copy the threatening look of the warrior, and the
triumphant expression of the victor?"

"Very much so."

"So the sculptor must give his statues a soul copied from life as well."

2. Painting (CA 369–375)

The remains of painting from the 5th. century, other than on vases, are exiguous
indeed. And yet it was highly considered among the arts, and the leading
practitioners like Zeuxis and Parrhasius had reputations quite as great as
Phidias. Most of its developments went hand-in-hand with those of vase-
painting; but the sources also suggest advances in the techniques of shading and
perspective which seem to have had little impact on the linear tradition of the
vase-painters.

CA 369 PLUTARCH, *Moralia* 345f–346a (*On whether Athens was more distinguished in peace or in war*)

345f   There are many arts of which Athens has been the mother and benevolent
nurse; some she has been the first to discover and propagate; to others she
has given weight and honour and expansion; but it is the art of painting to
which she has given the greatest advancement and distinction.

346a   For instance the painter Apollodorus who was the first to discover the
fading and gradations of colour values in shadow was an Athenian. It was
said of his works: "They are easier to denigrate than to imitate". And
there was Euphranor and Nicias and Asclepiodorus and Pleistaenetus,
brother of Phidias, some of whom painted victorious generals, others
battles or heroes.

CA 370 QUINTILIAN, *Oratorical Education* 12.10.3–5

3   The first painters of distinction whose works are remarkable not just for
their antiquity are said to be Polygnotus and Aglaophon. Their simple
colouring still has such ardent devotees that they prefer these almost
primitive works, the foundations of the art of the future, to the greatest of
their successors . . .

4   After that, Zeuxis and Parrhasius advanced the art considerably; they
were close in age, both working around the time of the Peloponnesian

5   War ... The former is said to have discovered the way of representing light and shade, the latter to have made a detailed study of line. Zeuxis emphasised the limbs of the body, thinking that this would give his work more grandeur and dignity ... Parrhasius' line-drawing was such that they call him "the codifier", because all other artists feel they have to imitate the pictures of gods and heroes that he made.

CA 371 PLINY, *Natural History* 35.54–69

54   Phidias himself was, we are told, initially a painter, and there is at Athens a shield painted by him ...

58   ... It was Polygnotus of Thasos who first painted women in transparent clothes, and gave them multi-coloured head-dresses; his major contribution was in freeing the face from its ancient rigidity by opening the mouth
59   and showing the teeth ... He painted the so-called *Stoa Poikilê* at Athens for nothing – part of it being done for a fee by Micon ...
60   Apollodorus of Athens attained distinction in the 93rd Olympiad (*408– 5*). He was the first to express the outward form of things, and really
61   confer glory on the brush ... He it was who first opened the gates of art by which Zeuxis entered ...
65   Zeuxis and Parrhasius are said to have resorted to a competition. Zeuxis exhibited some grapes painted so skilfully that birds flew into the picture; whereupon Parrhasius painted a curtain so true to life that Zeuxis, puffed up by the birds' verdict, now demanded that the curtain should be drawn and the picture revealed; when he realised his mistake, he conceded victory with proper deference ...
67   Parrhasius, a native of Ephesus, contributed much to painting; he was the first to introduce symmetry in the picture, minute detail in the face, elegance in the hair, beauty in the mouth, and is generally admitted by
69   artists to have been supreme in drawing outlines ... He painted "The Athenian Demos" in a most ingenious conception. He showed it as fickle, irritable, unprincipled, inconstant, while at the same time reasonable, lenient, compassionate, boastful, self-important and humble, fierce and timid all at once.

CA 372 ARISTOTLE, *Poetics* 1450a

Most young men's tragedies are not based on character and there are many such poets; much as among painters one can cite Zeuxis in comparison with Polygnotus: the latter was a good portrayer of character, but Zeuxis' painting lacks this quality.

CA 373 VITRUVIUS 7, *Preface* 11

Agatharchus was stage-manager for one of Aeschylus' plays at Athens and left a commentary about it. Following him Democritus and Anaxagoras wrote a work on the same subject to show how, if we take a fixed central point for the eyes to focus on and for the radii to be drawn from, then we must keep to the lines by a natural principle, so that indeterminate images on the painted scenery may provide us with the appearance of buildings, and things which are depicted on flat upright surfaces may appear to recede and project in different places.

CA 374 XENOPHON, *Memorabilia* 3.10.1–3, 5

1   For on one occasion when he was visiting Parrhasius the painter and was conversing with him, Socrates said, "Parrhasius, is not painting the making of a likeness of visible objects? At least you imitate bodies, whether they be concave or convex, shaded or light, hard or soft, rough or smooth, young or old, by making a likeness of them in colour."

2   "Quite right" answered Parrhasius.
     "Secondly" said Socrates, "when you portray beautiful shapes, as it is not easy to find one human being perfect in every respect, you assemble from many shapes the finest parts of each, and in this way you make bodies seem beautiful in every respect."

3   "Yes" said Parrhasius, "this is what we do."
     "Finally" said Socrates, "do you also imitate the character of the mind, at its most persuasive, most pleasing, most loving, most friendly and most

5   desirable? . . . Surely also nobility and generosity of mind, mean and servile characteristics, moderation and prudence, overbearingness and vulgarity show in human looks and gestures whether they stand still or are moving?"
     "Quite right" answered Parrhasius.

CA 375 XENOPHON, *Memorabilia* 3.11.1–2

1   There was once a beautiful woman in the city called Theodote, who distributed her favours freely. One of the company mentioned her, saying that she was more beautiful than words could convey; and that when artists were admitted to do likenesses of her, she revealed to them as much as was decorous.
     "Then we must go and see her" said Socrates; "we clearly cannot discover what words cannot convey just by listening."

2   "Come and follow me then" said the speaker. So they went to Theodote's house, and stood by watching while she posed for some painter or other.

VII. THE SCIENCES

(a) NATURAL SCIENCES

The Natural Scientists of the fifth century concentrated mostly on the fields of investigation already opened by Thales and the Milesian school. They were principally interested in the phenomenon of change, manifesting itself most obviously in the growth and decay of natural objects. Allied to this was the problem of knowledge: it could be shown that human perception was not infallible, and yet it remained our only source of evidence about the physical world; could it then be that we were totally mistaken about common-sense beliefs, and that all appearance of change was in fact illusory?

The leading scientist of the Periclean period was Anaxagoras of Clazomenae. His ideas may be seen as a reaction against those of Parmenides who had claimed that all change is impossible, since nothing can come into being from what is not already there. Anaxagoras accepted the premise, but got round the difficulty by postulating the existence of a bit of everything in everything: change was therefore simply a reshuffling of these constituent parts, thereby altering the appearance; the evidence of the senses was unreliable, but at least gave us an idea of the true nature of things. His cosmological ideas were somewhat more fanciful, and got him into trouble (see CA 295).

CA 376 ANAXAGORAS, fr. 17, 21, 21a

17   Things never come into being or are destroyed, but they are compounded of existing matter and dissolved into them.

21   The weakness of our senses makes us unable to determine the truth.

21a   Sight is the appearance of the imperceptible.

CA 377 THEOPHRASTUS, *On Sense* 27

Anaxagoras says that perception is by means of opposites . . . For a thing that has the same warmth or coldness does not make us warm or cold as it gets nearer, nor can we recognise sweetness and bitterness by means of themselves; but we recognise cold by warmth, drinking-water by brackish, sweetness by bitterness, according as each is deficient in us.

CA 378 AETIUS 1.3.5

Anaxagoras tried to show that the basic constituents of all matter were "homoeomeries" . . . We feed ourselves with nutriment that is simple and single in form, like bread and water, and from this is nourished our hair, veins, arteries, flesh, sinews, bones and all the other parts of the body. This being the case, it follows that there is, in the food we take in, everything that exists, and everything will grow from what exists. In that food there are particles which produce blood and sinews and bones and the rest – particles which only reason can apprehend.

CA 379 HIPPOLYTUS, *Refutation of Heresies* 1.8.3–10

3   He (Anaxagoras) says that the earth is flat and remains suspended because of its size, and because there is no void, and the air, which is very strong,

6   holds it up as it floats . . .; the sun, the moon and all the stars, are flaming

7   stones carried round by the rotation of the ether . . .; we cannot feel the heat of the stars because of their great distance from the earth; and they are not as hot as the sun because they are in a colder area; the moon is

8   below the sun and nearer to us; the sun exceeds the Peloponnese in size; the moon does not have its own light, but takes it from the sun; the stars

9   rotate under the earth; the moon is eclipsed when the earth, or sometimes the bodies under the moon, get in the way; the sun is eclipsed when the

10   new moon is in the way . . . He said that the moon was earth-like and had
      plains and ravines on it.

CA 380 DIODORUS SICULUS 1.7.1–7

(Rival cosmological theories are being considered)

1   According to them, at the original formation of the universe, both heaven
      and earth looked alike, as their characters were blended; later, when their
      bodies separated from one another, the universe adopted the whole of its
      present visible arrangement; the air took on constant movement, and the
      fiery part of it collected into the highest regions, as anything of this sort
      has a rising tendency because of its lightness, for which reason the sun and
      the rest of the abundance of stars were included in the general whirl, while
      what was muddy and turbid, having a moist consistency, settled into one
2   spot because of its weight, and continually revolving upon itself and
      becoming compressed, out of the wet is made the sea, out of what was
3   more stable the land, which was clayey and entirely soft. This first of all
      acquired firmness as the sun's fire shone down, then, as its surface was
      fermenting because of the heat, parts of the wet formed swellings in many
      places, and about them pustules surrounded with delicate membranes
      developed, just as is still now seen to occur in marshes and swampy
      regions, whenever the land has become cold but the air becomes very hot
      suddenly without making the change gradually.
4   While the wet was having life engendered within it through the heat in
      the manner described, at night things immediately received their suste-
      nance from the mist that fell from the surrounding air, while by day they
      were made firm by the burning heat; and finally when the embryos had
      obtained their complete growth and the membranes had been heated right
5   through and broken open, there grew up all forms of living creatures. Of
      these, those that had shared the most heat became winged and went off to
      the high regions, while those that clung to earthy consistency were
      counted in the class of crawling things and the other land creatures, while
      those who had partaken most of the wet character gathered into the
6   regions of similar character, taking the name of aquatic creatures. As the
      earth always grew firmer because of the sun's fire and the winds it finally
      was no longer able to generate any of the larger creatures, but every kind
      of living thing was begotten by interbreeding.
7   It seems that with regard to the nature of the universe even Euripides,
      who was a pupil of the natural philosopher Anaxagoras, does not
      contradict the above arguments, for in his *Melanippe* he put it like this:
           "For heaven and earth were once a single form;
           But since they were divided from each other,
           All things they now do bear and bring to light,
           Trees, birds, and beasts, and what the salt sea breeds,
           And the human race."

(b) MATHEMATICS (CA 381–383)

Mathematical understanding had been much advanced in the fifth century by
the arithmetical work of Pythagoras and his school, on proportion and the

properties of number; the concept of "odd" and "even", and "square" numbers, probably originate from them. Their other interest was in the solving of geometrical problems (like doubling the cube and squaring the circle), and the formulation of proofs. In Athens there does not seem to have been a particularly strong interest in Mathematics before the fourth century, although the problem of squaring the circle was well enough known to find its way into comedy (CA 337).

CA 381 PHILOPONUS, *Commentary on Aristotle's Physics* A2

Hippocrates of Chios was a merchant who, after falling in with a pirate ship and losing all his possessions, came to Athens to bring a suit against the pirates. As the suit entailed a long stay in Athens, he frequented philosophical circles, and attained such proficiency in geometry that he tried to find a way of squaring the circle. He was unsuccessful; after squaring the lune (*the space included by two arcs*), he thought wrongly that he could work out how to square the circle.

He was also one of those who tried to find a method of doubling the volume of a cube (see I. Thomas: *Greek Mathematical Works*, vol. 1. pp. 257ff).

CA 382 PLUTARCH, *Moralia* 607e–f (*On Exile*)

No situation can take away from man his happiness, his virtue or his intelligence: when Anaxagoras was in prison, he wrote about squaring the circle.

CA 383 THEMISTIUS, *Commentary on Aristotle's Physics* A2

(*Themistius dismisses Hippocrates' attempt to square the circle*) . . . But the geometer could not say anything against Antiphon, who inscribed an equilateral triangle inside the circle, and on each side of it put another isosceles triangle with its apex on the circumference of the circle; he thought that if he went on drawing triangles like this, in the end the side of the last triangle, straight though it was, would coincide with the circumference.

(c) MEDICINE (CA 384–393)

The greatest scientific advances were made in medicine – not so much in diagnosis and treatment as in approach. Among the new generation of doctors led by Hippocrates of Cos, and perhaps influenced by sophistic thinking, disease was regarded as a natural phenomenon with natural causes. The first need was to find out more about it, not to postulate sweeping and fanciful hypotheses. To this end detailed case histories were collected so that accurate prognosis could be made about the course of the illness. Such methodology is evident in Thucydides' account of the Plague (2.48.3–50). Notions about the origins of disease however remained beset by preconceptions about the effect of external climatic conditions and internal "humours", and for obtaining a cure, supernatural aid in the form of prayer and sacrifice, or the wearing of charms

(CA 271) or "incubation" in the Temple of Asclepius, was still thought to be indispensable.

CA 384 PLATO, *Gorgias* 500e–501a

501 I was saying that cookery does not seem to me an art but an empirical skill, whereas medicine is an art since it has studied the nature of what it is tending and the rationale of what it is doing and can give a detailed explanation of this.

CA 385 HIPPOCRATES, *Ancient Medicine* 20

In my opinion a clear understanding of natural science can only come from Medicine. When a man has a proper grasp of Medicine, and not till then, he can understand it, and give accurate answers to questions like "What is Man? From what causes does he come?", and so on.

CA 386 HIPPOCRATES, *Ancient Medicine* 1–2

All those who have undertaken to speak or write about Medicine have manifestly been in error by postulating some hypothesis as the basis of their argument – like heat or cold or wetness or dryness or anything else they fancy – restricting the initial causes of disease and death among men to one or two postulates, the same ones in each case. This is particularly reprehensible in that Medicine is an art which everyone uses in important situations, and whose best practitioners are held in highest regard . . .

. . . So I say that Medicine has no need of the empty hypotheses which are required if one is going to say anything about invisible mysteries like what is up in the sky or under the earth . . .

2   But Medicine has long had all its material available, and an established principle and method, which has resulted in many fine discoveries over a long period, and which will lead to the discovery of the rest if the person is competent and uses the earlier discoveries as the basis of his own investigation.

CA 387 HIPOCRATES, *Prognostic* 1

It seems to me a very good thing for the doctor to practise prognosis. For if he can discover and tell the patients in advance what is likely to happen, as well as past and present symptoms, and supply the information that the patient has omitted, he is more likely to be thought to understand the patients' condition, and to win their complete trust. And besides, his treatment would be most effective if based on foreknowledge of the consequences of the present symptoms.

CA 388 HIPPOCRATES, *Epidemics 1 Case 10*

Man from Clazomenae, lying by the well of Phrynichides, caught fever; pain in the head, neck, groin to begin with, then deafness; insomnia, high fever; some abdominal swelling and distension; dry tongue. 4th. day: delirium at night. 5th. day: suffering distress. 6th. day: all symptoms intensified. Around the 11th. day, slight improvement. From the beginning until the 14th. day, thin plentiful watery bowel motions, but not causing trouble to the patient. Then constipation. Urine throughout thin, but of a good colour, containing much suspended matter which was not precipitated. Around the 16th. day, the urine was a little thicker and contained a little sediment; the patient was more comfortable and clearer in his mind. 17th. day: urine thin again; painful swelling at each ear; insomnia, delirium, pain in the legs. 20th. day: crisis: no fever, no sweating, patient quite rational. Around 27th. day, severe pain in the right hip, quickly subsiding; the ears neither recovered not suppurated, but continued painful. Around the 31st. day: copious watery diarrhoea like dysentery; thick urine; the ears recovered. On the 40th. day, pain in the right eye, with some blurring of vision. The patient recovered.

CA 389 HIPPOCRATES, *On the Nature of Man* 4

The body of man contains in itself blood and phlegm and yellow and black bile, and these are the constituents of the nature of the body, and the causes of pain and good health. A man has the best health when these elements are properly related to one other in terms of mixture, strength and quantity, and are perfectly fused together; he suffers pain when there is a deficiency or surplus of any of them, or one of them is isolated in the body and not mixed in with all the rest.

CA 390 HIPPOCRATES, *Airs, Waters, Places* 1

Anyone who wants to pursue Medicine properly should act as follows: first consider the seasons of the year and their different effects, . . . then the winds hot and cold, principally the ones generally found, and in particular the ones prevailing in each locality. He must also consider the properties of the waters, which differ considerably in respect of taste and weight. So when a man comes to an unfamiliar city, he should consider its situation in relation to the winds and the rising of the sun.

CA 391 DIODORUS SICULUS 12.58.3–5

(*The Plague at Athens in 430*)

3   As heavy rains had fallen during the preceding winter, it resulted that the soil became waterlogged, and many hollows in the ground, on receiving a quantity of water, became marshy and acquired standing water like swampy places; when these were collected up in summer and became stagnant, thick foul-smelling vapours collected, and when these rose as steam they polluted the atmosphere nearby; just as is seen to occur on

4   swamps when they are pestilential. What contributed to the plague too was the low quality of the food supply imported; for during that year the crops became quite sodden and were spoiled. A third cause of the disease happened to be the failure of the North Trade winds, through which most of the heat regularly cools in the summertime; as the warmth became intense and the atmosphere became scorching, people's bodies came to be

5   injured if no cooling occurred. That is why at that time all diseases turned out to be inflammatory, because of the excessive heat. For this reason

most of the sufferers from the plague would throw themselves into wells and fountains, wanting to cool their bodies.

CA 392 ARISTOPHANES, *Wealth 406–412, 653–663*

(*In an Athens poverty-stricken by the loss of the war against Sparta, Chremylus and Blepsidemus come across the blind figure of Wealth and seek to restore his sight*)

BLEPSIDEMUS. Then hadn't we better fetch a doctor?

CHREMYLUS. Where can one find any doctor in the city nowadays? Without any fees there's no medicine.

BLEPSIDEMUS. Let's keep our eyes open.

CHREMYLUS. But there isn't one.

BLEPSIDEMUS. No, you're right.

410   CHREMYLUS. No, but the best thing is to do what I planned before – make him spend the night in the temple of Asclepius.

(*This they do, and later Wealth's slave Carion describes how his master was cured*)

CARION. As soon as we reached the god, bringing the wretched man – as he then was, though now as blessed and fortunate as anyone – first of all we took him to the sea and bathed him . . .

660   . . . Then we went to the precinct of the god, and when we had offered cakes and preparatory sacrifices on the altar, a honey-cake to the flame of Hephaestus, we laid Wealth down to sleep in the regular way; and each of us patched up a mattress for ourselves.

(*Later in the night the god made a round of his patients and prescribed treatment; Wealth was cured by the magical powers of two holy serpents who licked his eyes*)

CA 393 *IG* IV² 121.4

(*From the record of cures in the temple of Asclepius at Epidaurus; late 4th. century*)

Ambrosia from Athens, blind in one eye. She came as a suppliant to the god; going round the shrine she laughed at some of the cures as being incredible and impossible – that people who were lame or blind should be cured just by seeing a dream. But when she slept there she saw a vision; the god seemed to stand over her and say that he would cure her, but in payment she would have to make an offering of a silver pig as a memorial to her stupidity; after saying this he operated on her diseased eye and poured a drug into it. And when day came she left the temple cured.

(d) RHETORIC (CA 394–405)

The ability to speak in public had always been important in Greek life, but only in the fifth century did it come to be regarded as a science with its own discipline, as new techniques were developed and publicised by the sophists (see CA 209 ff.). Such professionalism not only posed a threat to democracy – since it gave an advantage to those who could afford to pay for expensive courses in Rhetoric – but it also brought with it a moral danger by setting a higher value on persuasion than on truth. Popular prejudice regarded it as liable to pervert justice by making the weaker argument appear the stronger (see CA 218). The art was further embellished at the end of the century by the refinement of sound effects and cadences.

CA 394 XENOPHON, *Memorabilia* 3.3.11

Socrates, discussing the qualities needed by a cavalry-commander, suggests that among other things, he ought to be a good speaker.

"Has it never occurred to you that we learn through speech all the principles of life which convention has taught us to be the best ones, as well as all the other worthwhile lessons; that the best teachers use speech most, and the greatest experts in matters of the greatest importance use discussion most?"

CA 395 PLATO, *Phaedrus* 266d–267e

PHAEDRUS. There is a lot of detail, Socrates, in the treatises written on the art of speaking.

SOCRATES. I'm glad you reminded me. First I think they tell us there should be an "introduction" at the beginning of a speech. That's the sort of technical detail you mean, isn't it?

e PHAEDRUS. Yes.

SOCRATES. Secondly there should be an "expository narrative", supported by "direct evidence"; thirdly "circumstantial evidence"; fourthly "probabilities"; and I think the Byzantine word-wizard talked of "confirmation" and "reconfirmation".

PHAEDRUS. You mean the excellent Theodorus?

267 SOCRATES. I do indeed. And he said that one should employ "refutation" and "rerefutation" in both prosecution and defence. We won't bring the splendid Evenus of Paros into the ring, who first invented "innuendo" and "insinuated praise" – some say that he actually delivered his "side-swipes" in metre to make them more memorable: he was a clever man. And shall we leave Tisias and Gorgias in peace, who saw that probabilities were more valuable than the truth and can make

b little appear big and big little by force of argument, and utter new things in an old way or old things in a new, and discovered both consciseness and infinite length in handling every topic? Once when I was telling Prodicus all this he laughed and claimed that he himself alone had discovered the art of right argument: neither length nor brevity, he said, was required but proportion.

PHAEDRUS. Good for you, Prodicus.

SOCRATES. And what about Hippias? I think our Elian friend would vote with Prodicus: . . . And how about Polus' thesaurus of expressions, like

c "word-repetition" and "maxim-coining" and "figure-coining", and the names which Licymnius gave to Prodicus for the creation of fine language?

PHAEDRUS. Weren't Protagoras' expressions of much this sort?

SOCRATES. Yes, he contributed "word-correctness" and many other good ones. But I think our Chalcedonian friend had in particular mastered the art of pulling out all the stops of piteous language in dealing with

old-age and poverty; he was also very clever at incensing a large audience all together and then charming them back again by "casting a
d   spell on them" as he used to say; and he was superb both at making false accusations or dealing with them from any quarter. As to the conclusion of a speech all the experts seem to agree, whether they call it "recapitulation" or some other name.

PHAEDRUS. You mean that they finally at the end of a speech make a summary to remind their audience what they have said?

SOCRATES. Yes – and that's about it, unless you have something to add?

PHAEDRUS. Nothing of importance.

CA 396 PLATO, *Cratylus* 384b

SOCRATES. There is an old proverb which says that the true nature of beautiful things is hard to discover: and this whole problem of names is a difficult one. If I had heard Prodicus' 50-drachma lecture-course which he claims provides a complete education on the subject, you could have the truth of the matter right away: as it is, I haven't heard it, but only the 1-drachma course; so I'm still in the dark.

CA 397 PLATO, *Euthydemus* 277e

Now you must regard yourself as listening to the first of the Sophistic rites. For first, as Prodicus says, one must learn about the correctness of names.

Gorgias:

CA 398 DIODORUS SICULUS 12.53.2–4

(*The people of Leontini in Sicily send an embassy to Athens in 427*)

2   The leader of this delegation was Gorgias the orator, who far excelled his contemporaries in subtlety of speech. He was the first person to make a science out of rhetoric, and as a sophist teacher he was so outstanding that
3   he could charge his pupils 100 minas. When he first arrived and was brought before the assembly, he made a speech about the alliance, and he astonished the Athenians by the strangeness of his style, although they
4   were naturally clever and literary. For he was the first to employ configurations of speech to a rather extravagant degree, which excelled in ingenuity, antithesis of sentences with equal units exactly balanced and ending in the same syllables, and so on – methods which at the time because of the strangeness of the treatment were granted approval, but now seem to be pedantic and appear ridiculous when employed too frequently.

CA 399 PLATO, *Gorgias* 452d–e

SOCRATES. ... What do you claim is that greatest good for mankind of which you are the artificer?

GORGIAS. The truly greatest good of all, Socrates, responsible alike for the freedom of mankind and the individual's power to control others in his city.

SOCRATES. What is it?

e   GORGIAS. The power to persuade by words the jury in the law-courts, the
     councillors in the Council, the audience in the Assembly, in short any
     public meeting. This power will make your doctor and trainer alike the
     slave of the man who wields it; and the businessman you were talking
     about will be seen to be doing business not for himself but for you – the
     man who can speak and persuade the masses.

CA 400 PLATO, *Gorgias* 459b–c

SOCRATES. So the ignorant will be more persuasive than the expert before
an ignorant audience, when you have the orator being more persuasive
than the doctor?
GORGIAS. In this instance, yes.
SOCRATES. Doesn't the orator and his rhetoric stand in just this relation to
all the other arts too? He doesn't need to know the facts but to have
c   discovered the trick of persuasion which will make the ignorant think
he knows more than the expert.
GORGIAS. Well isn't that a real luxury, Socrates, – without learning the
other arts but just this one, to come off no worse than the experts?

CA 401 GORGIAS fr. 11a. 35

If it was possible for the truth about events to become crystal-clear to an
audience by means of words, judgement based on oral evidence would
now be a simple matter. But this is not so.

Antiphon:

CA 402 PLUTARCH, *Moralia* 832 b–e (*Lives of the Ten Orators*)

Antiphon son of Sophilus of the Rhamnusian deme was instructed by his
c   father (a sophist whom Alcibiades used to go to for lessons as a boy, so it
is said). After acquiring the art of persuasion (through his own natural
gifts some think), he embarked upon a political career, but made use of his
spare time by involving himself in discussions with Socrates, not in any
combative spirit, but simply for the sake of arguing, as Xenophon has
recorded in his *Memorabilia*; he also wrote speeches for anyone who
wanted them for use in the law-courts. Some say he was the first to do this.
d   At any rate there are no forensic speeches either of his predecessors or of
his other contemporaries extant, because the practice of writing them
e   down had not yet been adopted . . . He was also the first to publicise
rhetorical techniques.
     (*Antiphon was a leader of the oligarchic revolution of 412–411, and after
its overthrow, when he was put on trial for his life he made 'what might be
thought the finest speech of defence ever yet known' (Thuc. 8.68.1–2)*)

CA 403 PLATO, *Menexenus* 235e–236a

e   MENEXENUS. Do you think you yourself could make such a speech if you
     had to and the Council chose you?
     SOCRATES. For me to be able to make a speech would not be surprising,
     Menexenus, since I was taught by a woman who was no mean hand at

rhetoric and numbered among the many good orators she produced one who was outstanding in Greece, Pericles the son of Xanthippus.

MENEXENUS. Who? You must mean Aspasia.

236   SOCRATES. I do, and also Connus the son of Metrobius. These two were my teachers, the one in music, the other in rhetoric. So there is nothing surprising about a man of my upbringing being good at speaking; but even someone worse educated and taught music by Lamprus and rhetoric by Antiphon of the deme Rhamnus could win fame by praising Athenians before an Athenian audience.

CA 404 ARISTOTLE, *Rhetoric* 1402b

... This amounts to "making the worse appear the better argument". And this is why people justly criticised Protagoras' prospectus. It is both deceptive, involving apparent but not real probability, and based not on genuine art but on rhetoric and eristic.

CA 405 CICERO, *Orator* 174–5

Isocrates' principal admirers give him the greatest credit for being the first
175   to introduce rhythmical cadences into prose ... But this is somewhat less than the whole truth. For though one must concede that no-one was better versed in this technique than Isocrates, yet its original inventor was Thrasymachus, whose extant writings are in fact rhythmical to the point of excess.

(e) HISTORIOGRAPHY (CA 406–409)

The first scientific historian is usually regarded as being Thucydides, and certainly his exacting standards of accuracy and impartiality (Thuc.1.20–22) and his powers of analysis could not be matched by any other ancient historian except perhaps Polybius. However, credit in the development of historiography should also be given to Herodotus who is far from being just the credulous story-teller that critics suggest. Considering the range of his subject and the intractability of his sources, he exercised exemplary care and considerable acumen in gathering his information (see e.g. 2.19–25, 73, 99; 7.152) and conscious art in the presentation of it.

CA 406 CICERO, *On the Orator* 2.55–56

(The speaker is maintaining that the most eloquent of the Greeks devoted themselves to writing rather than advocacy)

55   Herodotus, who was the first to give distinction to historical writing, was, we understand, never engaged in lawsuits; and yet his eloquence is such as
56   to give great pleasure to me, in so far as I can understand Greek. And after him Thucydides was in my opinion outstanding for his virtuosity of style: his material is so rich that the number of ideas almost equals the number of words, and his language is so exact and condensed that it is hard to tell

whether the material is embellished by the style or the language by the ideas.

CA 407 DIONYSIUS OF HALICARNASSUS, *On Thucydides* 5

(*A large number of historians who came before Thucydides are listed by name* . . .) These all adopted a similar policy in their selection of material, and were very much the same in ability. Some wrote Greek histories, others Barbarian, but rather than fitting them together, they kept them separated by countries or states, and set them out individually. They kept one and the same end in view, to make common knowledge of whatever records were preserved among the inhabitants of different countries or states, whether these were deposited in sacred or public places, and to add or subtract nothing from what they recorded, even though this included legends believed in for many generations, and dramatic stories of reversals of fortune which nowadays seem very silly. For the most part they all adopted the same style – where they used the same dialect –, one that was clear, conversational, pure and concise, suitable to its material and exhibiting no elaboration of technique.

CA 408 EUSEBIUS, *Evangelical Preparation* 10.3.16

(*Quoting Porphyry Bk.I*)

Herodotus in Book II borrowed many passages almost verbatim from Hecataeus of Miletus – for instance the description of the phoenix and the hippopotamus, and hunting crocodiles.

CA 409 MARCELLINUS, *Life of Thucydides* 22, 36

22   His teacher in philosophy was Anaxagoras (*see Index*), from whom he imbibed the theories which led to his being thought something of an atheist . . .; he was also a pupil of the orator Antiphon, a man skilled in rhetorical technique (*see CA 402–3*) . . .

36   Up to a point he affected the balanced phrases and antithetical vocabulary of Gorgias of Leontini (*see CA 398–401*) which were highly regarded in Greece at the time; and on the other hand the precision of terminology associated with Prodicus of Ceos (*see CA 395–7*).

VIII. PHILOSOPHY

(a) *NOMOS* AND *PHYSIS* (CA 410–422)

Apart from the topics mentioned in chapter VII a, most philosophical debate resulted from the polarisation of the concepts of *nomos* and *physis*. *Nomos* is a word meaning "that which is believed in"; and the basis of authority for this belief may be mere convention, or the divine will (the "unwritten laws" of CA 251–3), or man-made legislation; it is the word for "law" and for "custom". Whereas *nomos* results from attitudes consciously adopted by man, or attributed by him to God, *physis* represents instinct and the laws of nature; it is man's character in its elemental state. The concepts diverge further as scepticism increases about the role of God in determining human behaviour, and the fields of debate in which the controversy is most apparent are (1) *religious* – whether gods exist in nature or merely by convention (see CA 274 ff.); (2) *moral* – what principles should determine man's relation to man; and (3) *political* – how states should conduct themselves towards each other. The upholder of *nomos* maintains that law is a necessary constituent of human society, and that progress is impossible without it (this is implicit in Pericles' remarks about the laws in Thuc. 2.37); necessarily he must also admit that different societies require different laws, and that moral values are therefore relative and not constant (the point is nicely illustrated by Herodotus' story of different burial habits in 3.38, concluding with the tag from Pindar, that "*Nomos* is Lord of all"). The upholder of *physis* claims that values are constant, as human nature is everywhere the same: all actions spring from the same instincts, mainly those of self-interest, and therefore should be judged in the same light. In its most trenchant form this becomes an assertion of the right of the strong to oppress the weak (see particularly Thucydides on the Athenian Empire, 1.76.2; and on the Melian debate, 5.104.3–105).

Upholders of *Nomos*:

CA 410 EURIPIDES, *Suppliants* 429–437

> THESEUS. Nothing is more inimical to a city than a tyrant: first of all there are no common laws, but one person has taken sole possession of the law, and that is the end of equality. But when there are written laws, the
> 435 weak and the wealthy have justice in equal measure, and you can get equal redress for defamation, whether a leading citizen or less powerful, and the weaker can defeat the stronger if he has justice on his side.

CA 411 ANONYMOUS WRITER (probably late 5th. century) quoted in the *Protrepticus* of Iamblichus p.100 (DK II p.402)

> Furthermore one should not launch oneself on the path of aggrandisement, nor think that virtue lies in using force for aggrandisement, and that obedience to the laws is cowardice. For this is the most depraved idea, and gives rise to all that is the opposite of good, namely wickedness and harm. For men are incapable of living on their own but have yielded to necessity and banded themselves together; their whole life and civilisation is based on this, inasmuch as it is impossible to live in a state of lawlessness when they are banded together – for this would incur an even greater handicap than the solitary life. So all these factors make it inevitable that law and justice should rule among men and remain immutable; for they are firmly secured by nature.

CA 412 XENOPHON, *Memorabilia* 4.4.12–13

> (*Hippias to Socrates*)

> 12   "Are you saying, Socrates, that law and justice are the same thing?"
> 13   "I am".
>   "I don't see what you mean by law and justice."
>   "You know what I mean by state-laws?"
>   "I do."
>   "What do you think they are?"

"A written code agreed by the citizens about what they should and should not do."

"So the citizen who abides by it would be acting lawfully, and he who transgresses it, unlawfully."

"Certainly."

"And if a person obeys the laws, he would be acting justly, and if he disobeys them unjustly, is unjust."

"Of course."

"So the law-abiding man is just and the lawless are unjust."

CA 413 EURIPIDES, *Suppliants* 201–213

THESEUS. I praise that deity who transformed our mode of life from the chaotic and bestial to an orderly state, first giving it the power of understanding, then a tongue to convey the intelligible sounds of
205   speech; and the fruit of the earth for food, and rain-drops from heaven for its nurture and germination; and shelter from storms, protection
210   from clear open skies; and passages over the sea, that we might barter with others for what our own countries lack. And what is not evident and open to understanding, diviners interpret from examination of fire and the folds of entrails and the flight of birds.

CA 414 DIOGENES LAERTIUS 2.16

(*Archelaus, Socrates' teacher*)

He was called the scientist, because scientific study stopped with him, once Socrates had introduced ethics. It seems though that he too took a part in ethics. For indeed he has speculated on the laws and right and justice. From him Socrates inherited this interest, but because he developed it to its peak was assumed to have been the inventor. He used to say that there were two causes of becoming, heat and cold. Also that living things were created from slime; and that justice and immorality were determined not by nature but convention.

Relativity of values:

CA 415 EURIPIDES, *Phoenician Women* 499–502

ETEOCLES. If everyone had the same views on goodness and wisdom, there would be no disputatious strife among men. But as it is, nothing is the same or equal, except in name – in reality, nothing.

CA 416 PLATO, *Protagoras* 333d–334c

(*Socrates and Protagoras speaking*)

"You agree that there are such things as good things?"
"Yes."
"Are those things good which are beneficial to man?"
e   "Certainly. And I call good even things which are not beneficial to man."

I thought that Protagoras had become a bit tetchy and upset by this point and had taken up battle-stations; so seeing him in this state I asked

cautiously and mildly: "Do you mean, Protagoras, things which are
334   beneficial to no human, or things which bring no benefit at all? Do you call
even the latter good?"

"Not at all. I know many things which are harmful to men – food,
drinks and medicines and lots of other things – but yet have their uses; and
some which are neither harmful nor useful to men, but are to horses; some
which are useful only to cattle, others to dogs; some to none of these, but
to trees; some which are good for the roots of trees, but bad for the shoots,
b   as for instance dung; . . . and olive-oil is very bad for all growing things
and for the hair of all other creatures apart from man, whereas for a man's
hair and his whole body it is a stand-by. Good is such a many-coloured
c   and many-sided thing, that even in the case of olive-oil what is good for a
man's external parts is ruinous for his insides: thus all doctors forbid sick
people the use of more than a drop of olive-oil in their diet – just enough
to kill the unpleasantness to the senses through the nostrils that can arise
from food."

CA 417 PLATO, *Theaetetus* 151e–152a

SOCRATES. I think what you have just said about knowledge is no trivial
152   utterance but something Protagoras also used to say. He has said the
same thing a different way. He says somewhere that man is "the
measure of all things – of their existence or non-existence". Have you
read that somewhere?

THEAETETUS. I have often read it.

SOCRATES. Doesn't he mean, more or less, that as things appear to me, so
they are to me, and as they appear to you, so they are to you? And by
"man" he means individuals like you and me, doesn't he?

THEAETETUS. Yes.

Upholders of *Physis*:

CA 418 PLATO, *Laws* 889e–890a

What is more there is no correspondence, they say, between what is
naturally admirable and what is conventionally so. As for natural
morality, there is no such thing, but morality is a matter of constant
890   argument and change. Any change is sovereign for the moment, resulting
as it does from contrivance and conventions and no natural cause. All
this, my friends, is the creed of clever men, whether laymen or poets,
presented to the young – a claim that morality is whatever a man can
make prevail by force; and so you find all sorts of irreverence besetting the
young, on the grounds that the gods in whom the law enjoins belief do not
exist, and the result is division in society because they are pulled towards
the "naturally" correct life, namely a life of dominance over others rather
than "servility" to one's fellows under the law.

CA 419 ARISTOPHANES, *Clouds* 1420–1429

(*Phidippides is defending his proposition that sons have a right to beat their
fathers*)

STREPSIADES. But it's totally against the law to treat fathers like this.

PHIDIPPIDES. Was it not a man like you and me who made this law in the first place by persuading our forefathers in argument? So haven't I got just as much right now to make a counter-proposal giving sons the right to beat their fathers in turn? As for the beatings received before this law is passed, we'll discount them, and give you them for nothing. But look at your cock-roosters, and the rest of the animal kingdom, look how they fight their fathers; and yet how do we differ from them, except that they don't pass formal decrees?

CA 420 ANTIPHON (*Sophist*), fr. 44

(*From a work on Truth*)

Justice then consists in not transgressing the conventions (*nomima*) of the city in which one is a citizen. So a man would make the most advantageous use of justice if he were to regard as important the laws when witnesses are present, but nature when he is on his own. For the demands of law are artificial while those of nature are inescapable, and the demands of the laws are the result of agreement, not natural growth, while those of nature are the opposite. So a man who breaks the conventions without being seen by the people who drew them up is free of shame and punishment – but not if he is seen. But if anyone tries to do the impossible and defy what is established by nature, he comes to grief no less if no one sees him, and no more if everyone does. For his downfall is brought about not by opinion but by truth. It is just that that forms the object of my inquiry, to show that many of the things that are legally justified are at variance with nature.

CA 421 PLATO, *Republic* 338e–339a

(*Thrasymachus is defending his proposition that "justice is the interest of the stronger party"*)

Each form of government lays down laws that are to its own advantage – a democracy democratic laws, a tyranny tyrannical laws, and so on; after laying them down they make it clear that for those who are governed justice is simply what is in the government's interest, and they punish anyone who transgresses as a lawbreaker and wrongdoer. So that, my friend, is what I mean when I say that justice is the same thing in all states, 339a namely the interest of the established government. This is the ruling force everywhere; so the proper logical conclusion is that justice is everywhere the same, namely the interest of the stronger party.

CA 422 PLATO, *Gorgias* 483c–484a

CALLICLES. Thus conventionally we call immoral and wrong the effort to
d   gain at the expense of the majority. But nature herself on the other hand makes it clear enough, I think, that it is right for the better to gain at the expense of the worse and the more capable at the expense of the less capable. She provides widespread evidence of the truth of this principle both in the animal world and in human societies and families – the principle that morality means the rule to their own advantage of

the strong over the weak. What other principle justified Xerxes'
e   campaign against Greece or his father's against the Scythians or
thousands of other similar actions? Nature is the justification: I would
go so far as to say it is a law of nature, but not perhaps the sort of law
we lay down for ourselves, licking into shape all the best and strongest
among us, getting hold of them when they are young, and taming them
484   like young lions with musical incantations and bamboozling them and
breaking their spirit by saying that men must have equal shares and this
is what is fine and moral. But, in my opinion, if a man is born with what
it takes, then he shakes off and breaks and escapes these fetters,
tramples on all our rule-books and mumbo-jumbo and solemn incantations and the whole unnatural paraphernalia of law, and this slave of
ours rises up and reveals himself as master, and there you have Nature's
morality in all its splendour.

(b) SOCRATES
1. Life (CA 423–427)

There is no doubt that the leading intellectual figure of the fifth century was
Socrates. No one attracted more biographical attention in antiquity, and no
one's name occurs more frequently in these pages. But for all that, there are
great areas of uncertainty about his life and work. He wrote nothing himself
(except some poems, Plato *Phaedo* 60d), and most of the biographical works,
published after his death, are coloured by the circumstances of his trial and
execution. The only contemporary picture, in Aristophanes' *Clouds*, is deliberately distorted; and in Plato's philosophical works it is impossible to tell at what
point the ideas attributed to Socrates come to represent Plato's own development of them. The other main source, Xenophon's *Memorabilia*, is probably an
accurate record of Socrates' opinions on a wide range of subjects, but the
treatment is fragmented, and far from providing a complete picture of the man.

From the information left to us we can be pretty sure of Socrates' military
record (showing him to be of the comparatively wealthy hoplite class), of his
refusal to be involved in politics except when he was a member of the *Boulê* just
after the battle of Arginusae in 406 (Plat. *Apol.* 32a–c), of his non-cooperation
with the Thirty Tyrants in 403 (ib.32c–d), and of his trial under the restored
democracy in 399. These are virtually the only known public events of his long
life. For his character we have more ample testimony: he was a man of
exceptional humanity and no pretensions; he was entirely master of himself and
susceptible to no external pressures or restraints; his presence was compelling
and his effect on others overwhelming.

CA 423 DIOGENES LAERTIUS 2.18, 19, 22–23

18   Socrates was the son of Sophroniscus, a stone-mason, and a midwife,
Phaenarete, according to Plato in the *Theaetetus*, an Athenian, from the
community of Alopece.
19   Duris says he was a slave and worked with stone; some say the Graces
on the Acropolis are his, being fully-clothed.
22   He kept in good training, and was in good physical shape. At any rate
he took part in the Amphipolis campaign (*422*), and when Xenophon fell

23   from his horse at the battle of Delium (*424*), he picked him up and rescued
him: when all the Athenians were in flight, he remained calm, turning
round to look and protecting himself against attack. He also served at
Potidaea (*432–0*), travelling there by sea, as the war prevented his journey
overland.

*(He may also have wanted to travel to Potidaea by sea so as to avoid going
through Thessaly, which he regarded as a lawless autocracy (Xenophon
Mem.1.2.24))*

CA 424 XENOPHON, *Memorabilia* 1.6.15

Once Antiphon asked him how he could think of making others into
politicians, when he wasn't a practising politician himself – however much
he might understand the subject. Socrates replied: "Would my involvement in politics be greater if I simply engaged in them on my own, or if I
worked to make as many others as possible capable of doing so?"

(For an example of Socrates' encouraging others in politics see CA 35).

CA 425 PLATO, *Symposium* 215c–216a

d   ALCIBIADES. You, Socrates, differ from Marsyas only in that you achieve
the same effect by the use of pure words without any instrument. At any
rate we can listen to someone else, excellent speaker though he may be,
uttering arguments other than yours and we remain all of us virtually
unconcerned: but when any of us listens to you or to your arguments in
another's mouth, however poor a speaker he is, man, woman and child
we are dumbfounded and entranced. Speaking for myself, gentlemen,
were it not that I should be thought completely tipsy, I should have
declared to you on oath what I have felt and still do feel under the
e   influence of Socrates' arguments. When I listen to him, my heart leaps
and the tears pour from my eyes at his words far more than is so with
the devotees of Cybele in their frenzy; and I know plenty of others have
the same experience: whereas when I listen to Pericles and other good
speakers, while admiring their skill, I had no such experience – my soul
was not put in a turmoil nor did I grow indignant at my slavish
216   condition. But this Marsyas here has often had this effect on me and
made me feel that life is not worth living in my present state.

*(Marsyas was a satyr, credited with great skill on the pipes. Apart from
the comparison here made, Socrates was said to look like him)*

CA 426 XENOPHON, *Memorabilia* 4.8.11

Of all those who knew what kind of man Socrates was, it was the seekers
of virtue who continue even now to miss him most, having found in him
the greatest help in cultivating virtue. For me he was just the sort of person
I have described – so religious as to do nothing without the gods'
approval; so just as to do no one the slightest harm, and all his
acquaintances the greatest good; so self-controlled as never to put
pleasure in front of goodness; so sagacious as never to make a mistake in
distinguishing good from bad, and never to need any help in making up
his own mind; able to expound and define such concepts; able to cross-

examine others, confute their errors of reasoning, and direct them towards goodness and virtue. In my opinion he was the model of a very good and very happy man. If you object to the idea, compare his character with anyone else, and then give me your verdict.

CA 427 PLATO, *Symposium* 221d–222a

(*The view of Alcibiades*)

221d He is such an extraordinary man, both for his personality and for his conversation, that it would be impossible to find anyone like him, either in the present or in the past, unless you liken him and his conversation, as I
e   have done, not to anything human, but to Silenus and the satyrs . . . If you decide to listen to Socrates' speech, it sounds quite ridiculous at first, such are the words and phrases that provide its outer covering, like the hide of a wanton satyr; he talks of pack-asses and blacksmiths and cobblers and tanners, and appears always to use them to say the same things, so
222a attracting the ridicule of people with no knowledge or sense. But when you really get inside his meaning and see his ideas expounded, you will find them uniquely sensible, divinely inspired, containing numerous images of virtue, and covering the widest possible range, including every subject suitable for study by anyone with pretensions to being a gentleman.

2. Socrates' Philosophy (CA 428–436)

Plato *Phaedo* 96a–98c tells us of the development of Socrates' philosophical interest in the problem of causation: how he found the explanations of the natural scientists inadequate, so turned to Anaxagoras' theory of Mind, and finally felt compelled to follow his own path of investigation. This intellectual independence led him to challenge established philosophical systems by rigorous dialectical argument, and to seek in their place a watertight logical basis for all moral concepts. To convince others of the importance of this quest, and of the need to "care for their souls" became his great mission in life (Plato *Apol.* 28d–30c).

The Socratic method:

CA 428 PLATO, *Republic* 487b–c

(*Adimantus to Socrates*) This is what your hearers are always experiencing: because of their unfamiliarity with the question-and-answer technique they feel that they are gradually led astray by each question, and when all of these gradual steps are put together at the end of the argument the conclusion is catastrophic and quite the reverse of their starting-point. They feel like the inexperienced player of *pessoi* (*cf. CA 471*) who at the end of the game is trapped by the expert and has nowhere to move his
c   pieces; so they are finally trapped by this so to speak *pessoi* game of yours and have nothing to say.

CA 429 PLATO, *Theaetetus* 150c–d

SOCRATES. I have this in common with midwives. I am myself barren of clever ideas, and the common reproach against me, that I question others but have nothing positive to say about anything because I have no clever ideas, is a fair one. The reason is that God compels me to be a midwife but has debarred me from giving birth. So I am myself not at all clever and my mind has not given birth to any clever discovery: but those who converse with me even if at first some of them are obviously extremely ignorant, none the less all as the conversations proceed make – God permitting – marvellous progress both in their own eyes and the eyes of others; and it is quite clear that they achieve this not by learning anything from me but by discovering from themselves and giving birth to many excellent ideas.

d

CA 430 CICERO, *Tusculan Disputations* 5.10

Up to the time of Socrates, who had sat at the feet of Archelaus (*cf. CA 414*), a pupil of Anaxagoras, ancient philosophy was concerned with numbers and movements, and the origins and destinations of everything; earnest enquiry was made into the size, intervals, courses and everything about the heavenly bodies. Socrates was the first to bring philosophy down to earth: he located it in the cities of men, even brought it into their homes, and made people think about life and morals, and what is good and bad.

(*For the topics of Socrates' conversation, see CA 26*)

CA 431 ARISTOTLE, *Metaphysics* 1078b

Socrates was concerned with the moral virtues and was the first to try to reach general definitions of them ... Two discoveries we can justly attribute to Socrates – inductive arguments and definitions: both belong to the root of knowledge. But Socrates did not make his universals or definitions separable from particulars ...

The idea that Virtue is knowledge:

CA 432 PLATO, *Meno* 70a–71b

70   MENO. Can you tell me, Socrates, whether virtue is something teachable? or is it not teachable but attained by practice? or is it neither, coming to men rather by nature or some other means?

SOCRATES. Meno, the Thessalians have long been famous and the envy of other Greeks for their horsemanship and their wealth, but now, it
b   seems, they are famous for their cleverness too, not least the Larisians of your friend Aristippus. You have Gorgias to thank for this, who came to Larisa and captured as intellectual lovers the leading Aleuadae (among them your lover Aristippus) and the leaders among the other
c   Thessalians. What is more he accustomed you, as befits those who know, to answer questions fearlessly and spectacularly, just as he himself offered himself to the Greeks for questioning on any subject and always gave an answer. But here in Athens, my dear Meno, the
71   opposite has happened and there is a sort of drought of cleverness. It must have all flowed your way. At any rate if you want to ask this sort of question to people here, everyone will laugh and say "My friend, you may think I am a wonder – or at least that I know whether virtue is

teachable or comes by some other means; but so far am I from knowing whether it is teachable or not that I don't even know at all what virtue is".

b   And that's my condition too, Meno. I share my fellow-citizens' dearth of this commodity, and indict myself of complete ignorance about virtue. And if I don't know what it is, how can I know what sort of a thing it is? or do you think that if someone doesn't know at all who Meno is, he can know whether he is handsome or rich or noble, or the opposite of all these? Is it possible, do you think?

CA 433 ARISTOTLE, *Eudemian Ethics* 1216b

Socrates in his old age thought the true objective was understanding virtue, and he sought to discover what morality is and what courage is and what their constituent parts are. This was rational of him, since he thought that all the virtues were forms of knowledge and that people became moral simultaneously with understanding morality, just as we are geometers or builders as soon as we have learnt geometry or building. Thus Socrates sought to find out what virtue is, but not how it arises or from what cause.

CA 434 XENOPHON, *Memorabilia* 3.9.5

Socrates said that justice and every other form of virtue is wisdom; for every just or virtuous action is fine and good; and people who know how to do them would not choose to do anything else instead (while people who do not know are unable to, and fail if they try); so fine and good things are done by wise people (while those who are not wise are unable to do them, or fail if they try); therefore since every just or otherwise fine and good action is virtuous, it is clear that justice and every other form of virtue is wisdom.

CA 435 PLATO, *Protagoras* 345d–e

(*Socrates speaking*)

My belief is more or less this, that no clever man thinks any man errs willingly or willingly commits shameful and evil deeds, but is convinced all men only do so involuntarily.

A critical view:

CA 436 XENOPHON, *Memorabilia* 1.6.11–12

11   On another occasion, when Antiphon (the Sophist) was conversing with Socrates, he said; "Socrates, I do indeed reckon you to be a just man, but not in any way wise. In fact you seem to recognise this yourself, as you do
12   not charge anyone a fee for associating with you ... You may indeed be just, in that you don't deceive anyone by profiteering, but wise you cannot be, as what you know is valueless."

3. Socrates' Trial and Execution (CA 437–449)

Plato's *Apology* is our principal source for the trial of Socrates. Although we cannot be sure of its historical authenticity, it is of particular interest in suggesting that Socrates took little trouble over refuting the actual charges: only in chapters 24–27 and 33 does he deal with them in specific terms, and the major charge of religious unorthodoxy is unconvincingly side-stepped. He is more concerned with dispelling prejudices against him, particularly those originating from Comedy (e.g. Aristophanes, *Clouds*, and CA 338), and with justifying his life-work. This in turn suggests that the real weight of the prosecution did not lie in the actual terms of the indictment. One of the lost works on Socrates appearing in the 390s was the *Accusation* of Polycrates: it is highly probable that this included the political charges which Xenophon takes pains to refute in detail, and which figure in many later sources. Under the amnesty of 403 Socrates could not be tried for political offences; but even so it is likely that his disparaging views on Athenian democracy (see Plato *Protag.* 319a–320b, *Gorg.* 515c–e, Xen. *Mem.* 3.5.13–22: LACTOR 5, pp.30, 14, 44), his approval of oligarchy (see e.g. Plato *Crito* 52e–53a), and his association with dangerous men like Alcibiades and Critias attracted more hostility from a government sensitive about its position than did his religious scepticism which many shared. See Plato, *7th. Letter* 325b–c, LACTOR 5 p.54.

The accusers:

CA 437 DIOGENES LAERTIUS 2.40

The affidavit in the case was as follows (it is still preserved, says Favorinus, in the Metroon): "This is the indictment and affidavit made by Meletus the son of Meletus of Pitthus, against Socrates the son of Sophroniscus of Alopece: Socrates is guilty of not recognising the gods recognised by the state, but of introducing other new divinities: he is also guilty of corrupting the youth. The penalty claimed is death."

On Meletus see Plato, *Euthyphro* 2b; the other prosecutors were Anytus and Lycon.

CA 438 DIODORUS SICULUS 13. 64.6

(An incident from Anytus' past life (409))

The Athenian people sent out to help those blockaded thirty ships under the command of Anytus son of Anthemion. He set sail then, and because of some storms was unable to round Malea, so he returned to Athens. The people were angry at this, accused him of treason, and referred him for trial. But Anytus though in acute danger saved his own life with money, and is thought to have been the first Athenian to bribe a jury.

CA 439 ARISTOTLE, *Constitution of Athens* 34.3

The terms of the peace (*404*) being that the Athenians should operate their hereditary constitution, the popular party tried to preserve democracy. The aristocrats were divided: those in political clubs and some of the exiles who returned after the peace wanted oligarchy; but those who belonged to no club but otherwise were of equal repute to any of their fellow citizens tried to establish the hereditary constitution. Among the latter were

Archinus, Anytus, Clitophon, Phormisius and many others, but their leader was Theramenes.

CA 440 ISOCRATES 18.23–24

23 He is well aware too that Thrasybulus and Anytus, despite being the most powerful men in the state and having been robbed of a large sum of money (*by the Thirty*), and knowing who registered it as state property, nevertheless have not the nerve to bring a law-suit or seek redress, but however
24 much more able they may be to attain their ends in other matters, in the matter of the terms of this agreement they regard themselves as on a level with everyone else.

Religious ideas:

CA 441 XENOPHON, *Memorabilia* 1.1.2

Socrates was often to be seen sacrificing at home or on the communal state altars, and he made no secret of his use of divination. In fact it was common knowledge that he claimed to receive signs from the deity – which in my opinion was principally responsible for his being charged with "introducing new deities".

For Socrates' private "deity", see Plato, *Apology* 31c–d.

CA 442 XENOPHON, *Memorabilia* 1.1.11

No one ever knew Socrates to do or say anything that offended against piety and religion. He even avoided discussing the popular topic of cosmology . . . making it clear that anyone who devoted his mind to such a thing was a fool.

He was also scornful of "scandalous tales about the gods" (Plato, *Euthyphro* 6a).

CA 443 ARISTOPHANES, *Clouds* 830–837

(*Strepsiades is reproaching his son for not knowing that Dinos has taken over from Zeus (cf. CA 286)*)

PHIDIPPIDES. Who says so?
STREPSIADES. Socrates the Melian, and Chaerephon who knows about flea-tracks.
PHIDIPPIDES. Are you so out of your mind as to believe lunatics like that?
STREPSIADES. Mind what you say; don't write off clever and intelligent people like that – they're so thrifty that none of them ever shaves or anoints himself or goes to the bath for a wash.
(*The epithet "Melian" links Socrates with the atheistic ideas of Diagoras (cf. CA 290–1). Chaerephon's experiments with fleas are described in Clouds 143–52*).

The political accusations:

CA 444 ISOCRATES 11.4—5

4 Realising that you (Polycrates) are far from preening yourself on your *Defence of Busiris* or your *Accusation of Socrates*, I will try to make it
5 quite clear to you that you went far astray in both speeches . . . In your

attempt to accuse Socrates, as if meaning rather to praise him, you granted him Alcibiades as one of his disciples, a man whom nobody saw being taught by him but on whose outstanding abilities everyone would agree.

CA 445 ARISTOTLE, *Constitution of Athens* 39.6

The political amnesty of 403:

It was decreed that no-one should be allowed to bring up a grievance about the past against anyone, except against the Thirty, the Ten, the Eleven or the Governors of Piraeus, and not even against them if they agreed to a public examination of their record.

CA 446 XENOPHON, *Memorabilia* 1.2.9, 12, 49, 56

9   Socrates' accuser maintained that he made his followers despise the established laws by saying that it was ridiculous to choose the city's rulers by lot, when you wouldn't think of using a helmsman or a builder or a piper chosen by lot, people whose mistakes would do much less harm than mistakes in government. It was such arguments, the accuser said, which led the young to despise the established constitution and become violent.

12   The accuser said: Critias and Alcibiades were both associates of Socrates, and both did the greatest harm to the state.

49   The accuser said: Socrates taught people to treat their fathers with contempt by persuading them that he made his followers wiser than their fathers.

56   The accuser said that he also picked out particularly immoral passages from the most celebrated poets, and by citing them as evidence persuaded his followers to espouse wickedness and tyranny.

CA 447 AESCHINES 1.173

You, men of Athens, put Socrates, the sophist, to death because he had clearly educated Critias, one of the Thirty who overthrew the democracy . . .

CA 448 PLUTARCH, *Cato the Elder* 23.1

(*Plutarch cites this among many instances of Cato's rabid anti-Hellenism*)

Cato said that Socrates was an overbearing chatterer who tried as best he could to become tyrant of his country, by destroying its traditions, and by persuading his fellow-citizens to adopt ideas contrary to the laws.

A suggestion that Socrates offered no defence:

CA 449 PLATO, *Gorgias* 486a–b

(*Callicles speaking to Socrates*)

If at this moment someone laid hands on you or any other philosopher and lugged you off to prison on a false charge, you know you wouldn't
b   know what to do but would be bewildered and struck dumb, and going before the court and being accused by an utterly worthless accuser, you would be put to death if he chose to ask for this penalty.

IX. SPORT AND RECREATION

(a) ATHLETICS (CA 450–470)

Physical fitness was part of the Greek ideal, and had an important place in the educational system. The traditional justification for it was military, but many, like Socrates, valued it for its own sake, and there was the further incentive of athletic competition. The Olympic Games had attracted competitors from all over Greece since the eighth century; two hundred years later similar Games were instituted at Delphi, Corinth and Nemea. Finally in 566 Athens decided to enlarge the scope of her Panathenaic festival by the addition of athletic competitions once every four years. Besides the standard events (running, wrestling, boxing, pancration and pentathlon), there were various forms of horse-racing, and a number of curious competitions with ritualistic origins, both for teams and for individuals. The wrestling-schools (palaestras) and gymnasia offered facilities for practising these skills, as well as for non-competitive activities like playing ball-games and knuckle-bones (see CA 202).

The cult of athleticism and its critics (see also Aristophanes *Clouds* 961ff., LACTOR 5 p.28–29):

CA 450 PLATO, *Protagoras* 342a–c

Philosophy is most longstanding and most extensive among the Greeks in
b   Crete and Sparta, and most of the world's Sophists are there. But they deny it and pretend to be stupid, to conceal the fact that they are cleverer than other Greeks ... Instead they pretend they prevail by fighting and courage, thinking that if they gave away the secret of their supremacy, cleverness, others would practise it. As it is, they hide their light under a bushel, and have deceived their imitators in other cities, who play the
c   Spartan by getting their ears bashed and wearing boxing-thongs and going in for physical exercise and wearing short cloaks, as if this were the recipe for Spartan supremacy.

CA 451 XENOPHON, *Symposium* 2.17

Socrates is laughed at for saying that he would like to take lessons from a Syracusan dancer who has just been giving an acrobatic display in which all parts of the body were active.

"Are you laughing at me because I want to improve my health, my appetite and my sleeping by exercises of this kind, and because I don't want to be like a long distance runner whose legs grow strong while his shoulders dwindle, or like a boxer whose shoulders are strengthened while his legs grow spindly, but rather by exercising all parts of the body to make it all equally strong?"

CA 452 XENOPHON, *Memorabilia* 3.12.1–2, 4–5

1   Seeing the poor physical condition of one of his companions, a young man called Epigenes, Socrates said: "What bad training your body is in."
    "That's because I don't need to be in training."

"Yes you do, just as much as an Olympic competitor. Or do you regard
as unimportant the fight for life which the Athenians will undertake
2 against their enemies sometime or other? I tell you there are plenty of
people whose physical degeneracy has been responsible for their death –
4 or at least inglorious survival – among the hazards of war . . . People with
bodies in good condition fare just the opposite from those with bad: they
are healthy and strong; they are able to save their lives honourably from
the hazards of war and escape all disasters; many of them help their
friends and serve their country, thereby winning thanks, glory, and the
highest honours, which make the rest of their own lives more congenial,
5 and afford a better start in life to their children. The fact that the city does
not undertake military training publicly should make the individual more
rather than less keen to practise it himself."

CA 453 XENOPHON, *Memorabilia* 3.3.12–13

Have you never reflected that whenever a chorus represents this city – like
the one sent to Delos – none of the others from other states can compete
with it; nor can you find a company to compare in manliness with
13 ours? . . . And yet it is not in beautiful singing, nor in physical size and
strength that the Athenians excel, so much as love of distinction
(*philotimia*).

(*Delos was the scene of a four-yearly festival. "Manliness" was one of the
team events in the Panathenaea – see below*)

CA 454 EURIPIDES, *Autolycus* (fr. 282)

1 There are ten thousand things wrong in Greece, but none is worse than the
16 race of athletes . . . For who has ever helped his native city by winning a
prize for wrestling or running fast or throwing a discus or hitting someone
20 squarely on the chin? Will they fight the enemy discus in hand, or kick
them out of the country like so many footballs?

The Panathenaic Games (for detailed description see H. W. Parke: *Festivals of
the Athenians* pp. 33–50):

CA 455 ARISTOTLE, *Constitution of Athens* 60.3

The prizes in the Panathenaic Games are distributed to the victors by the
games-organisers (*athlothetae*): for the winners of music competitions
there are golden vessels and silver coin, shields for the manliness competition, and olive-oil for gymnastics and horse-racing.

CA 456 *Greek Anthology* 13.19

Nicoladas the Corinthian set up this statue; he was victor in the foot-race
at Delphi, and won five consecutive victories in the Panathenaic Games,
with jars of olive-oil for prizes . . . (*details of other victories follow*).

CA 457 *SIG* 1055

(*record of prizes in the Panathenaea c.400–350*)

. . . For singers with lyre accompaniment: 1st. prize – a golden garland,
1000dr., silver, 500; 2nd. – 1200; 3rd. – 600; 4th. – 400; 5th. – 300. For men

singing with pipe accompaniment: 1st. – a crown, 300; 2nd. – 100. For men playing the lyre: 1st. – a crown, 300; 2nd. (. . .) 3rd. – 100. For pipers: 1st. – a crown (. . .) . . .

For the winner of the boys' running race: amphoras of olive oil, 50; 2nd. – 10. For the winner of the boys' pentathlon: amphoras of olive oil, 30; 2nd. – 6. (. . . *and similar prizes for the boys' wrestling, boxing and pancration; there was also a category of "beardless youths" who competed for slightly larger prizes of olive-oil; and a series of horse-races with and without chariots*).

CA 458 XENOPHON, *Symposium* 1.2

(*This is how Xenophon begins the narrative of his Symposium*)

It was the time of the horse-race at the Great Panathenaea, and Callias the son of Hipponicus happened to be in love with young Autolycus who had just won the pancration; so Callias had brought him along to watch as well.

(*The Pancration was the most violent of the physical combat sports, involving boxing as well as wrestling, and sometimes ending in death*)

CA 459 ARISTOPHANES, *Birds* 291–292, with Scholiast

PISTHETAERUS. But what are these birds doing with such crests on? Are they competitors for the two-lap race (*diaulos*)?
Scholiast: This is because competitors in the *diaulos* wore crested helmets on their heads.

CA 460 PAUSANIAS 1.30.2

There is in the Academy an altar to Prometheus from which they run to the Acropolis with burning torches. The aim of the contest is to keep the torch alight throughout the race; if a man comes in first with his torch out, he forfeits his victory to the second runner; if his is out as well, then the third man is the winner; and if none of the torches is alight, no one wins.

CA 461 ARISTOPHANES, *Frogs* 1087–1095

AESCHYLUS (*contemptuous of the decadence of the modern, Euripidean, generation*). Nowadays no one is fit enough to carry the torch.
1089 DIONYSUS. You're right, by Zeus; I laughed myself dry at the Panathenaea when some fat, pale-faced slowcoach was running along bent double; he was lagging behind and doing badly. Then the people from the Potters' Quarter at the gates slapped him with the flat of their hands on
1096   the belly, the ribs, the flanks, the buttocks; under the blows, he let out a little fart, and fled, fanning the torch (*or* "with his torch extinguished").

CA 462 ARISTOTLE, *On the Gait of Animals* 705a

That is why pentathletes jump further when holding jumping-weights than when not, and runners run faster when swinging their arms.

(*The events of the pentathlon were: jumping, running, wrestling, and the throwing of the discus and the javelin. Jumping-weights are described in Pausanias 5.26.3*)

CA 463 PLATO, *Lovers* 135e

Have I got the hang of what you mean by a philosopher? You seem to be saying that they are like the pentathletes in comparison with runners and wrestlers in the athletic contests, where the pentathletes come second to these experts in their specialist contests but come ahead of the other athletes.

CA 464 AESCHYLUS, *Eumenides* 589–590, with Scholiast

CHORUS. That's one round to us.
ORESTES. But you can't boast that you've beaten me yet.
   Scholiast: This metaphor is taken from wrestlers who only concede defeat when thrown three times.

CA 465 ARISTOPHANES, *Knights* 569–573

(*The Chorus of Knights eulogises the gallantry of their ancestors*)

CHORUS. None of them ever troubled to count the number of the enemy, but they were the embodiment of defiance; and if ever they fell onto their shoulder in battle, they would wipe it clean, and swear they had never fallen, but carry on with the contest.

CA 466 PLUTARCH, *Alcibiades* 2.2

When Alcibiades was getting the worst of a wrestling bout, he set his teeth in his opponent's arm to stop himself being thrown, hard enough to bite it clean through. The other loosened his hold and said: "You're biting, like a woman".
   "No" said Alcibiades, "like a lion."

Athletic training:

CA 467 ANTIPHON 3.2.3–4

3   I supposed that in teaching my son such a publicly useful skill, I should bring benefit to both of us. How wrong I was! In no spirit of wanton negligence but while practising javelin-throwing with his fellows in the gymnasium he did not hit or kill anyone in the proper meaning of the word, but another boy imperilled himself and my son became accidentally
4   involved in a charge of murder... The other boy ran in the path of the javelin and put his body in the way: so my son could not hit his target.

CA 468 PLATO, *Laws* 830a–c

Take the training of boxers... Would we go straight into a fight without any previous daily sparring? Of course not. As boxers we should work
b   hard at practice for weeks before the fight, trying out all the ploys we

intended to use in the battle for victory, and coming as close as possible to
the real thing, we should wear padded balls instead of boxing-thongs to
practise our attack and defence as realistically as possible; and if we had
an inadequate supply of sparring-partners, fear of the jeers of the ignorant
would not deter us from hanging up a lifeless dummy and practising
c   against that; and in the complete absence of opponents, live or dummy, we
should not be afraid to go in for actual shadow-boxing against ourselves.

CA 469 PLUTARCH, *Moralia* 38b (*On Proper Hearing*)

Xenocrates suggests that it is children rather than athletes who should
have ear-muffs fitted, as their whole character may be damaged by the
speech they hear, whereas the athletes are only likely to get a cauliflower
ear.

CA 470 EUSTATHIUS 1553.63 (Commentary on Homer, *Odyssey* 6.115)

It is said that among nations the keenest on ball-games were the
Spartans . . . among individuals, the poet Sophocles. When he was putting
on his play *The Washerwomen*, he was highly acclaimed for his performance in the part of Nausicaa playing ball.

(b) RECREATION (CA 471–481)

The non-athletic recreations of the Athenians were mostly of a simple kind,
though there may have been some sophistication in the game of *pessoi*. Many of
them were simply for amusement, like the variety of games and entertainments
that accompanied a large-scale banquet. But the favourite of all was probably
just sitting around in shops and other meeting-places exchanging talk and
gossip. And that is one thing that has remained unchanged for twenty-four
centuries.

CA 471 POLLUX 9.97–98

97   (The game of *pessoi*) . . . Each player has five pieces on five lines . . . The
98   middle line is called "the sanctuary". Moving your piece from there gives
us the saying: "to move from the sanctuary."
      The game with many pieces has a board with squares arranged in lines;
the board is called "the city", and each of the pieces is called a "dog"; the
pieces are divided into two different colours, and the art of the game is to
take a piece of the opposite colour, by trapping it with two of your own.

CA 472 ARISTOPHANES, *Wealth* 816–817, with Scholiast

(*Carion the servant describes the changes brought about by a sudden influx
of wealth into the household*)

CARION. We servants now play at Odd and Even with gold staters.

Scholiast: We hide the coins in one fist and ask the other player: "Have I got an odd or even number in my hand?" If he gets the answer right, he takes the coins; if he fails, he pays out that amount.

CA 473 AELIAN, *Varied History* 2.28

After the Persian wars, the Athenians instituted the custom of holding cock-fights in the theatre once a year.

The bizarre sport of "quail-flicking", mentioned in Aristophanes *Birds* 1299:

CA 474 POLLUX 9.107

One person would set the quail up; then the other would flick it with his forefinger, or pluck out the feathers from its head. If the quail stayed still, victory went to the person who had bred it; if it failed to do so and tried to escape, the flicker or plucker won.

CA 475 PLATO, *Theaetetus* 146a

SOCRATES. Which of us is going to be first to say (what knowledge is)? Whoever goes wrong over this or at any stage of the argument shall sit down, as the children say in their ball-games, as "donkey"; and whoever survives without a mistake shall be "king" over us and order us to answer any question he chooses.

Banqueting:

CA 476 ARISTOPHANES, *Wasps* 1208–1222

(*Philocleon (= Love-Cleon) is being taught how to behave in polite society by Bdelycleon (= Hate-Cleon). The setting is imagined*)

BDELYCLEON. Come and recline here and learn how to behave at *Symposia* and Get Togethers.

1210 PHILOCLEON. How should I recline then? Come on, tell me.

BDELYCLEON. Elegantly.

PHILOCLEON. Like this you mean?

BDELYCLEON. Oh *no*!

PHILOCLEON. How then?

BDELYCLEON. Straighten your knees, and pour yourself athletically like water over the coverlets. Then praise one of the bronze ornaments,

1216 examine the ceiling, admire the tapestries in the hall. Now then – Water for our hands! Bring in the tables! Dinner is served, We've had our wash. Now we pour libations.

PHILOCLEON. Heavens, is this a dream-banquet?

1219 BDELYCLEON. The pipe-girl has started playing. Your drinking companions are Theorus, Aeschines, Phanus, Cleon, and Acestor's son, a foreigner, at your head. See that you take up the drinking-songs (*skolia*) nicely with them.

CA 477 XENOPHON, *Symposium* 1.7–8

7 Socrates' party at first politely declined the invitation, as was to be expected, and did not promise to dine with Callias; but when he seemed very upset that they would not come with him, they did accompany him.

8   Then some of them took exercise and had a rub-down, and others had a
     bath too, before they presented themselves at his house. Autolycus sat by
     his father, and the rest, as you might expect, reclined.

CA 478 XENOPHON, *Symposium* 2.1, 2.11, 7.2, 9.2–4

*(Space does not permit us to reproduce in full Xenophon's detailed account
of a banquet, but here are some of the entertainments offered)*

2.1   When the tables had been taken away and they had poured a libation and
       sung a thanksgiving, a fellow from Syracuse came on for their entertain-
       ment, with a fine pipe-girl and girl dancer of the sort that can do
       acrobatics, and a boy who was very handsome and also very good at lyre-
       playing and dancing. The man used to exhibit their performances as if at a
       circus, and to get money for it.

2.11   After this a hoop was brought in stuck all round with swords standing
        on end; into the middle of these and out again the girl dancer somer-
        saulted, over the tops of the swords, so that the spectators were afraid that
        something would happen to her; but she boldly carried off the trick
        without a slip.

7.2   When Socrates had finished, they brought the girl dancer a potter's
       wheel, on which she was going to perform marvellous tricks.

9.2   After this, first a throne was set down in the room, and then the
       Syracusan came in and said: "Gentlemen, Ariadne will come into the
       chamber which is for her and Dionysus; after that Dionysus, who has been
       drinking rather a lot with the gods, will come and go in to her, and then
       they will play together."

9.3   After that, first Ariadne appeared, dressed as a bride, and sat down on
       the throne. Before Dionysus appeared the Bacchic rhythm was played on
       the pipes. Then the audience were filled with admiration for the dancing-
       master; for as soon as Ariadne heard the music she acted in a way that
       everyone would know she was delighted to hear it. She did not go to meet
       Dionysus, or even stand up, but it was clear that she could scarcely keep

9.4   still. When Dionysus saw her, he danced towards her, sat himself on her
       knees very lovingly, put his arms round her and kissed. She seemed to be
       abashed, yet lovingly embraced him in return. Seeing this, the guests at the
       banquet kept clapping and at the same time called out "Encore".

The game of *Cottabus*:

CA 479 Scholiast on ARISTOPHANES, *Peace* 343

There was a long stick fixed in the ground and another pivoted on top of
it, like a yoke on a yoke-pole; this had a pan fitted to either end, and
underneath each pan a bowl of water. Under the water-level stood a gilded
statuette of bronze. This was the arrangement at *symposia*: every competitor would take a cup full of wine and standing at a distance would
shoot all the wine in a single cascade into the pan; the pan thus weighted

down fell onto the head of the underwater statuette and made it ring. If it
overflowed with wine, he would win and know that his girl loved him.

Conversation, a national pastime:

CA 480 PLUTARCH, *Nicias* 12.1

Not only the young men in the wrestling-grounds but also the old men
sitting together in the workshops and meeting-places were sketching the
outline of Sicily and the appearance of the sea around it, and the harbours
and areas where the island faces Libya.

CA 481 LYSIAS 24.19–20

19 They further claim that there collects at my shop a ruffianly crew, men
who have spent their own money and scheme against the thrifty. You
know well that this accusation could be brought with equal justice against
20 any other tradesman. You are all in the habit of going to the spice-seller's
or the barber's or the cobbler's or what you will – the nearer the market-
place the more popular the gathering-place. So any charge of villainy
against my visitors will obviously apply equally to loiterers elsewhere – in
fact to all Athenians. You are all in the habit of loitering somewhere or
other.

INDEX OF NAMES AND SUBJECTS

The numbers refer to excerpts.
Names marked * appear also in the list of authors.